Leadership

# Leadership

## Strategic Thinking, Decision Making, Communication, and Relationship Building

ANN M. MARTIN and
KATHLEEN RIOPELLE ROBERTS

ALA Editions

CHICAGO | 2019

AASL

American Association
of School Librarians

TRANSFORMING LEARNING

**ANN M. MARTIN** most recently worked as the educational specialist for the Library Services Department of Henrico County Public Schools in Henrico, Virginia. Ann is a mentor in the Lilead Fellows Program. Ann has received many awards, including the 2011 AASL National School Library of the Year award for the district. She is a past president of the American Association of School Librarians (AASL) and is author of the book *Empowering Leadership*.

**KATHLEEN RIOPELLE ROBERTS** is the school librarian at Rivers Edge Elementary School in Henrico County, Virginia. She was an ALA Emerging Leader. She was a member of the AASL Standards and Guidelines Editorial Board, creating the *National School Library Standards* and presenting a webinar to support the book. Kathleen was selected as a candidate on the Fulbright Specialist Roster from 2018 to 2021.

© 2019 by the American Library Association

Extensive effort has gone into ensuring the reliability of the information in this book; however, the publisher makes no warranty, express or implied, with respect to the material contained herein.

ISBNs
978-0-8389-1907-1 (paper)
978-0-8389-1921-7 (PDF)
978-0-8389-1619-3 (ePub)
978-0-8389-1922-4 (Kindle)

Library of Congress Control Number: 2019025838

Book design by Alejandra Diaz in the Utopia Std and Galano typefaces.

♾ This paper meets the requirements of ANSI/NISO Z39.48–1992 (R2009) (Permanence of Paper).

Printed in the United States of America
23  22  21  20  19      5  4  3  2  1

# CONTENTS

# ACKNOWLEDGMENTS

We are deeply grateful to the American Association of School Librarians (AASL) for updating the *National School Library Standards* that provide a vision for school librarians. The AASL Standards Integrated Frameworks gave us the opportunity to make the connection with leadership skills to foster best practice.

Writing this book has been an experience both internally challenging and rewarding. We would like to recognize and acknowledge the following individuals for assistance with this book:

- The AASL Standards and Guidelines Editorial Board, under the leadership of chair Marcia Mardis, for developing forward-thinking principles to guide the professional excellence of school libraries and school librarians.
- Stephanie Book and Jamie Santoro, editors for AASL and ALA, for their keen insight and ongoing support in bringing the vision of this book to life.
- School librarians' willingness to share their experiences that provided background examples and authentic evidence for the importance of school librarians.
- Henrico County (Virginia) Public Schools colleagues from the building level through the district level who promote and support the development of strong school librarians and their instructional impact on learners.
- Shannon Hyman, educational specialist for library services for Henrico County Public Schools (HCPS), for her assistance in obtaining permissions for use of HCPS data.

We also would like to thank our families, who were important in getting this book finished. Kathleen would like to thank Matt, Henry, and Sophie Roberts for their understanding of the time needed for research and writing. She would also like to thank her father, Rip Riopelle, for his excitement about this project. Ann would like to thank Charlie Martin for reading drafts and for making sure she stopped to eat while working on this process. Ann would also like to thank her children, Beth Fisher and Andy Martin, and their families for their encouragement and support during the writing of this book.

# INTRODUCTION

**Leadership and learning are indispensable to each other.**
—JOHN F. KENNEDY

The idea expressed by President Kennedy in the preceding quotation is essential to school librarians as they make daily decisions to service stakeholders, including learners, educators, parents, and community members, in the school library. School librarians service stakeholders by fulfilling five interconnected roles—leader, instructional partner, information specialist, teacher, and program administrator—and by designing instructional lessons, making appropriate resources accessible, and promoting ethical use of technology (AASL 2018a, 14–16). When the various stakeholders' needs are met, the impact of the school library is felt throughout the larger school community.

The AASL *National School Library Standards for Learners, School Librarians, and School Libraries,* published in 2018, gives school librarians revitalized standards with which to continue their own development of leadership and learning skills. There is a strong connection between the AASL Standards and leadership of the school library because the Standards are designed to guide school librarians' interactions with learners, educators, and stakeholders, as well as to help school librarians engage in effective professional practice (AASL 2018a, 3). The AASL Standards are anchored in Common Beliefs that are fundamental to the profession. The AASL Standards Integrated Frameworks are composed of six Shared Foundations and their Key Commitments, along with four Domains of learning, featuring Competencies or Alignments for Learners, School Librarians, and School Libraries. "This domain-based approach to organizing the standards ensures that school librarians are able to personalize their professional practice and growth, continuously tailoring their school library to local needs, their own strengths, and learners' benefit" (AASL 2018a, 16). This book clarifies how to add capacity to school librarians' overall leadership and management of the school library by revealing the scope of these integrated frameworks and all three sets of standards.

School librarians use the AASL Standards Frameworks for School Librarians and School Libraries to drive their motivation for developing strategic-thinking, decision-making, communication, and relationship-building skills. The frameworks best foster the development of these qualities to maximize the potential of the school librarian and the school library in their service to stakeholders. Each of the four parts of this book explains how critical Competencies and Alignments apply to school librarians by defining how the skill connects to the school library and by providing authentic examples of the skill in action. In an attempt to create deeper understanding of the AASL Standards, each part focuses on three Shared Foundations and one Domain that most effectively exemplify the particular skill and related Competencies and Alignments. The five roles of the school librarian dynamically combine with the Domains "to allow school librarians and learners to personalize their growth; this webbing of roles and Domains is illustrated" in figure I.1 (AASL 2018a, 16). These roles weave through the book to emphasize how to use the Domains to strengthen the school librarian's leadership. Finally, every section contains self-assessment tools to facilitate the implementation and strengthening of strategic thinking, decision making, communication, and relationship building.

**FIGURE I.1**

## School librarians' roles reflected through domains

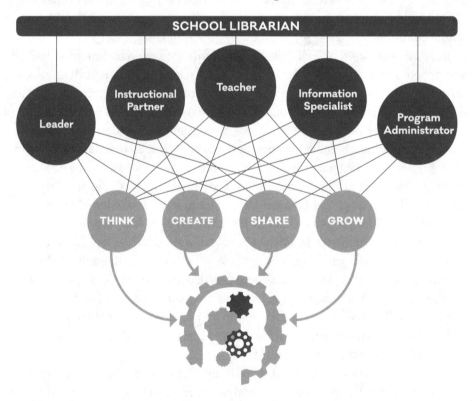

Source: Figure 1.4, AASL *National School Library Standards for Learners, School Librarians, and School Libraries,* standards.aasl.org, © 2018 American Library Association.

The focal point of part A, Strategic Thinking, is the Think Domain, which emphasizes the cognitive domain of learning. Using prior knowledge and new understanding provided by the AASL Common Beliefs, school librarians can construct a vision for the school library. The chapter on innovation translates an idea into an instructional plan and library service. By thinking through the logistics and then trying something new to benefit and enrich learners and educators, school librarians help their libraries stay relevant. To complete strategic thinking, school librarians must take the initiative, which requires asking questions, reflecting on the task, and implementing new ideas without hesitation.

Part B, Decision Making, exemplifies the Create Domain, which falls in the psychomotor sphere of learning. The chapters on problem solving, critical thinking, and emotional resilience require acquiring information and then putting it into practice. For example, problem solving uses information to create a process whereby specific steps result in successful outcomes to resolve issues. Critical thinking involves more complex reasoning that ends with modifications when drawing conclusions. And emotional resilience demands understanding of the why behind actions and then altering behaviors.

Part C, Communication, is an example of affective learning that is part of the Share Domain. Sharing knowledge and participating ethically are critical components of integrity. By aligning content and diverse viewpoints in formal and informal messages, the school librarian strengthens integrity by sharing knowledge that values stakeholder needs. Clarity refers to delivering information that is well thought out, without ambiguity, and relevant to the user. The chapter on delivery methods provides information about sharing messages after thoughtfully considering the most appropriate means for the intended audience.

Part D, Relationship Building, falls within the developmental learning of the Grow Domain. School librarians are professionals who value lifelong learning. The development of relationships that benefit the school library is an area of continuous growth that includes pursuing partnerships, developing self-awareness, and fostering stakeholder empowerment. The importance of creating partnerships for the school library includes recommendations about how to increase buy-in by stakeholders, resulting in more advocates who support change. School librarians discover the importance of knowing how their own perceptions and assumptions are at the center of relationship building. And the capstone for building relationships is growing stakeholder empowerment through shared responsibility. Coaching, mentoring, and delegating tasks are fundamental approaches for school librarians to engage in that foster their own empowerment while enabling stakeholder confidence-building.

School librarians must know how to interpret and use the AASL Standards effectively. This book breaks down the AASL Standards into authentic, easily accessible components that school librarians can apply to develop their leadership skills. Strategies, recommendations, and practical ideas for directing and managing the school library are supported by the Competencies and Alignments from the AASL Standards Frameworks for School Librarians and School Libraries. Reflective questions, assessment tools, and benchmark breakthroughs will bring school librarians to their next level in leadership development.

# Strategic Thinking

**W**hen librarians create transformational change for their library, success depends on developing a thoughtful game plan. School librarians start with a vision that creates relevance for the school library. This vision is based on solid beliefs and practices that advance the "core values that learners, school librarians, and school libraries should reflect and promote" (AASL 2018a, 17). The school library vision guides educators' and learners' futures by fostering inquiry, inclusion, collaboration, curation, exploration, and engagement. Developing innovative strategies to accomplish the vision is critical to improving processes, increasing efficiency and creating new services for learners and educators. In addition, school librarians push innovation forward by initiating action that integrates school library services and programs into the goals and objectives of the educational community the school library serves. The school librarian as leader positively influences the learning community by setting the groundwork that includes communicating change to stakeholders. This communication strengthens educators' and learners' understanding of the benefits that change brings to them as individuals. Strategic thinking that guides transformational change is basic to creating vision, being innovative, and taking initiative.

## A Strategic-Thinking Challenge for School Librarians

A common task often encountered by school librarians is the authentic integration of technology. Integration is a universal concern in which meeting the challenges of cost, hardware, and software merges with developing technology opportunities that strengthen educators' and learners' academic success. A variety of technology tools is available for school librarians to use to amplify their program, facilitate collaboration, and extend student learning. School librarians who make a conscious plan by formulating questions, reflecting on the resulting assumptions, and then engaging new uses of technology through collaborative outreach will create a more innovative yet relevant technology path. This example ties into the concept of strategic thinking because solving new technology integration proposals for the school library requires vision, innovation, and initiative. Savvy school librarians realize that relevance and school library growth are achieved by incorporating the Shared Foundations from the *National School Library Standards* when creating strategic plans. This section highlights best practices associated with the Domain Think in the Shared Foundations of Inquire, Collaborate, and Explore in the AASL Standards Frameworks for School Librarians and School Libraries. Strategic thinking is foundational for addressing technology integration and creating continuous and long-term success for the school library.

# Vision

There is no denying that vision is important to us as individuals. Vision, or eyesight, is used to interpret the world and enables people to see what is and decide how to react to situations. School librarians create a library vision that guides the librarian's goals for transformational change and reflects aspirations for the future of the school library. Think of the written vision statement as the keel on a sailboat. It guides the school library in unstable times or when the path ahead becomes unclear. Just as a keel holds the boat right side up in rough waters, the school library vision statement supports and strengthens the school librarian in times of transition.

A vision is more than just a statement. It is a reflection of the school librarian's ingenuity and a blueprint for change. In the *GE Annual Report 2000,* Jack Welch and his colleagues are credited with stating that "when the rate of change inside an institution becomes slower than the rate of change outside, the end is in sight" (p. 4).[1] School librarians must take responsibility to articulate stakeholder and school librarian ideas in the form of a vision to ensure that change within the school library exceeds the rate of change outside the school.

When developing a vision statement, following a set of common beliefs and foundational best practices creates connections between "learner, school librarian, and school library standards" (AASL 2018a). Essential to creating buy-in and understanding is to seek learner input. It is the school librarian who must be realistic about available financial and physical resources and guide the vision toward a practical result.

## Common Beliefs

When the American Association of School Librarians (AASL) began the evaluation and remodeling process for the *National School Library Standards,* the AASL Standards and Guidelines Editorial Board and KRC Research surveyed members and the profession to determine what school librarians felt were "qualities of well-prepared learners, effective school librarians, and dynamic school libraries" (AASL 2017–2018). The resulting Common Beliefs align with opinions held by members and the community. These Common Beliefs reflect "current learning practices and professional best practices" (AASL 2018a, 11). Based on the Common Beliefs, a set of standards composed of four Domains and six Shared Foundations was released.

A well-constructed school library vision is focused on the AASL Common Beliefs. The AASL *National School Library Standards* identified six Common Beliefs central to the profession (AASL 2018a, 11–14). The Common Beliefs form a balanced view of what school librarians need as a foundation for their vision of an effective school library. Filtering the vision through the concepts embraced in these beliefs ensures that the vision is aligned with school library best practices. When school librarians, serving as program administrator, apply these beliefs to a vision statement, they are preparing learners for the future and creating a dynamic school library.

### 1. The school library is a unique and essential part of a learning community.

When creating a vision statement, the school librarian characterizes the school library's purpose for learners by identifying the school library as a unique and essential part of the learning community. For example, a school librarian may determine that the school library serves as an extension of the classroom, that the school library is a lab-like space in which ideas and concepts are challenged, or that the school library provides a place for individualized research and learning. Perhaps all three characterizations might be true. School librarians take on the role of information specialist by providing and making accessible digital and print resources to all stakeholders—learners, educators, parents—and this function makes the school library a vital part of the learning community.

### 2. Qualified school librarians lead effective school libraries.

Essential to transformational change is leadership of the school library by qualified personnel. The role of the school librarian encompasses instruction, collaboration, and management. "To become a professionally qualified librarian, you [must have a master's degree] in librarianship or information science" (Cragg and Birkwood 2011). In their article entitled "Beyond Books: What It Takes to Be a 21st Century Librarian," Emma Cragg and Katie Birkwood (2011) explained that most people think of the librarian's job as stamping due dates in books. They went on to say that this perception persists because many people's experience is only with the frontline, customer service staff (Cragg and Birkwood 2011). School districts invest large amounts of revenue in the physical space and in the print and digital resources of a school library. Administering this space and maximizing library services requires professional personnel. Clearly identifying the need for a qualified school librarian is fundamental to a vision statement, particularly for schools in which staffing does not meet this requirement.

### 3. Learners should be prepared for college, career, and life.

School librarians are charged with preparing learners for their future vocation. School librarians embed a broad variety of instructional resources into curriculum content through collaboration with other educators. The relevant engaging learning opportunities resulting from the instructional partnership with educators are essential for creating lifelong learners. Interest and excitement are generated when learners search for and find information that answers authentic questions related to the curriculum yet connected to real life. Businesses, colleges, and the military need individuals who can share from their own knowledge and work together to solve problems. The school librarian prepares learners for their future endeavors by requiring group discussion in which diverse perspectives are considered. User-centered instructional and reading opportunities enable learners to practice career and life skills.

### 4. Reading is the core of personal and academic competency.

The more learners read, the more proficient they become in understanding the meaning behind what they read. Literacy goes beyond instruction, and school librarians know that reading for pleasure is important for learners to become proficient readers. As a result, school librarians select fiction and nonfiction materials, both print and digital, and champion reading promotions to draw learners into the library in an enjoyable way. School librarians know that when learners read topics of personal interest, their reading skills are sharpened as their reading time increases. Avid readers become confident readers who are more likely to succeed in every subject as well as to become proficient standardized test takers.

### 5. Intellectual freedom is every learner's right.

Open access to information is a basic right in a free society. This right means being able to read about multiple sides of an issue and make decisions based on the information received. Intellectual freedom is the right of learners to read information that is interesting and on an appropriate reading level. Intellectual freedom is typically viewed in the realm of reading, but access to information is also an intellectual freedom issue. Increased doorways to information through various social media and digital resources provide a free flow of information and ideas. The school librarian must emphasize ethical use of information as learners make choices about what they choose to read, view, and hear (AASL 2018a, 13).

### 6. Information technologies must be appropriately integrated and equitably available.

Because not every learner has access to up-to-date technology or digital resources, the school librarian serves a necessary role as information specialist by providing equitable access to information and innovative information technologies. To foster learners' success, access to the information they need must be available without limits. It is the responsibility of the school librarian as teacher and instructional partner to develop opportunities for authentic application and integration of resources and technology through well-designed lessons and deliberate collection decisions. Consistent opportunities for access allow learners to become experienced in incorporating technology to enhance learning.

## Connecting to the Shared Foundations

A vision is an outcome of strategic thinking. Strategic thinking is a process whereby, in this case, the school library is viewed and assessed as creating change. Strategic thinking results from developing and implementing specific skills, such as critical thinking, problem solving, and teamwork. These skills are reinforced in the Think Domain of the AASL Standards Frameworks for School Librarians and School Libraries and are specifically associated with the Shared Foundations of Inquire, Collaborate, and Explore. Effective strategic thinkers focus on these particular Shared Foundations in addition to the Common Beliefs to construct a strong and authentic vision statement to articulate the impact of the school library within the larger school community.

### INQUIRE

For school librarians, one of the fundamental tenets of Inquire is "activating learners' prior and background knowledge as context for constructing new meaning" (AASL 2018a, School Librarian I.A.2.). When creating a vision, the school librarian establishes the level of expectation based on past knowledge to decide the next level of goals, decisions, and best practices. The past knowledge and experiences could be focused on data reflecting resources available, use of physical space by the school, or the number of learners accessing materials, depending on the school library's needs. Building on past knowledge and experiences allows the school librarian to keep the vision realistic while being innovative and flexible to accommodate change in the school library.

"The school library enables curiosity and initiative by using a systematic instructional-development and information-search process in working with other educators to improve integration of the process into curriculum" (AASL 2018a, School Library I.A.2.). The focus of this Alignment is on working with other educators to follow an instructionally sound and resources-based process to create a vision for the school library, benefiting all stakeholders. An example of attaining this Alignment is collaboration with classroom educators in the instructional partner role to discuss how specific curriculum-based lessons incorporate school library resources. In another example, the school librarian as program administrator works with building-level administration to discuss how the physical and virtual school library spaces are organized to best meet the school's instructional needs. When the multiple facets of the school library are considered and discussed, the school library formulates a comprehensive vision.

## COLLABORATE

In the Shared Foundation of Collaborate, the Competency that stimulates the school librarian to develop a strong vision is "organizing learner groups for decision making and problem solving" (AASL 2018a, School Librarian III.A.3.). An effective vision respects diverse stakeholders' ideas and their needs. "Isolated instances, gut feelings, documented evidence, and irrefutable evidence provide opportunities for leaders to document support for improved practices" (Martin 2013, 161). By understanding user concerns, the school librarian can also identify common needs and goals to assimilate into the vision. Understanding how different stakeholders use school library resources becomes evident when the school librarian creates the opportunity to organize and then listen to learner groups. Learners, both staff and students, perceive the school library from different perspectives. In addition to learner input, the school librarian includes objectives to provide further options for the library's future. The final vision allows for maximum growth of the school library when the school librarian integrates stakeholder ideas, including the librarian's and those of the distinctive groups within the school. Thus, a variety of data gathering provides buy-in from users and rationale for transformational change.

When the school librarian uses an inquiry process to reach goals when working with other educators, the results reach farther in scope and depth. This idea is expanded to all stakeholders when "the school library facilitates opportunities to integrate collaborative and shared learning by leading inquiry-based learning opportunities that enhance the information, media, visual, and technical literacies of all members of the school community" (AASL 2018a, School Library III.A.2.). Enhancing and strengthening the necessary literacies of all members of the school community helps reach the vision of the school librarian to impact the larger school community. This Alignment can be realized with bigger events or through daily opportunities. A bigger occasion would be a literacy night hosted by the school library. When the school librarian designs and leads this literacy-focused night, in collaboration with learners and educators, for the community to build up literacies, the participants are becoming part of the school library's vision in action. The literacy night can include stations incorporating innovative technology, information resources, and multiple formats to create products so all members of the school community interact and develop new knowledge.

Daily inquiry-based learning opportunities, led by the school librarian, include formal instructional lessons, informal mentoring sessions, and conversations about choosing books for pleasure reading. Through these interactions, all members—learners, educators, and parents included—have the opportunity to strengthen their literacies through shared learning. The school librarian has a responsibility to consciously create these daily and bigger opportunities to amplify the school library's vision.

---

## EXPLORE

The school library serves many purposes in the school environment. Stakeholders—learners, educators, parents, and community members—have different expectations of the school library's services. The school librarian incorporates the Explore Shared Foundation into the vision by "challenging learners to reflect and question assumptions and possible misconceptions" (AASL 2018a, School Librarian V.A.2.). Because of these reflections and questions, the vision becomes much richer in scope and depth. Learners need the opportunity, directed by the professional school librarian as leader and program administrator, to reflect and question assumptions in order to expand their perception of the school library's role. Some examples of reflection opportunities are interviews or surveys, depending on the number of people to be reached. A school library committee representing all stakeholders then filters through the assumptions and misconceptions in order to develop key ideas for the school library's role in the larger school community. As the school librarian works with stakeholders to confirm and discuss common goals and aspirations, an authentic and strong vision begins to form.

Although part of the school librarian's responsibility is to develop a school library vision, the roles of leader, teacher, and program administrator focus on how to empower stakeholders to develop their individual visions with the support of the school library. This idea is stated in an Alignment: "The school library supports learners' personal curiosity by providing resources and strategies for inquiry-based processes" (AASL 2018a, School Library V.A.1.). Learners are not limited to students but also include educators in professional development sessions, collaborators in instructional lessons, and administrators analyzing school-wide data. When learners are made aware of how to access and review available school library resources and to deliberate strategies to construct their own visions, they are more interested in implementing the school library vision. Their investment in the school library becomes more real, and they appreciate the contributions of the school library to academic excellence.

## Sample Vision Statement

In the introduction to this section on strategic thinking, a need for authentic integration of technology was posed as an example of a current school challenge. Based on the AASL Common Beliefs and the Shared Foundations, the following may be a vision statement created by a school librarian who would like to implement transformational change specifically relating to authentic integration of technology.

> Within the next three years, the library will be the technology information center of the school. New and emerging resources that encourage collaboration and extend student learning will be evaluated, acquired, and equitably available to learners. Learners will develop the skills and competencies necessary to build a lifelong desire to seek answers to questions, pursue advanced study, and engage in satisfying professional work (AASL 2018, 12). Curation of current digital and print materials and technology will establish a culture of reading in the school community.

### Linking the Vision

Viewing the vision statement through the lens of the AASL Common Beliefs, Shared Foundations, and the Think Domain reveals connections that create a statement that is forward thinking and strategic.

- **Sentence 1:** Within the next three years, the library will be the technology information center of the school.
  - Relates to Common Belief 1. "The school library is a unique and essential part of a learning community" (AASL 2018a, 11).

- **Sentence 2:** New and emerging resources that encourage collaboration and extend student learning will be evaluated, acquired, and equitably available to learners.

- – Relates to Common Belief 6. "Information technologies must be appropriately integrated and equitably available" (AASL 2018a, 13).
- – Relates to School Librarian Competencies from the Shared Foundation Collaborate in the Domain of Think.

- **Sentence 3:** Learners will develop the skills and competencies necessary to build a lifelong desire to seek answers to questions, pursue advanced study, and engage in satisfying professional work (AASL 2018a, 12).
  - – Relates to Common Belief 3. "Learners should be prepared for college, career, and life" (AASL 2018a, 12).
  - – Relates to School Librarian Competencies from the Shared Foundation Inquire in the Domain of Think.

- **Sentence 4:** Curation of current digital and print materials and technology will establish a culture of reading in the school community.
  - – Relates to Common Belief 4. "Reading is the core of personal and academic competency" (AASL 2018a, 13).
  - – Relates to School Librarian Competencies from the Shared Foundation Explore in the Domain of Think.

## Establishing a School Library Vision

Everyone benefits from a guidebook to frame their professional goals. Astronaut Scott Kelly "stumbled across what would become a sort of guidebook for his life: *The Right Stuff* by the late novelist Tom Wolfe. . . . He felt connected to the test pilots that Wolfe described, and was inspired to become one himself—or maybe even to become an astronaut one day" (Breedon, 2018). Creating an authentic, strong vision for the school library requires intentional thought and guidance from a credible professional resource. The *National School Library Standards for Learners, School Librarians, and School Libraries* provides the Common Beliefs to use as a strong foundation and a guide for school library visioning.

Beginning with a current challenge, such as technology integration, and forming a vision to solve that issues are starting points when establishing a school library vision. After reviewing the AASL Common Beliefs, the next step in shaping a vision statement is for the school librarian to integrate appropriate School Librarian Competencies and School Library Alignments from the Shared Foundations of Inquire, Collaborate, and Explore that fall under the Domain of Think. Using these as filters means that specific lenses are applied through which the vision can be formatted and then implemented. Inquiring, thinking critically, and gaining knowledge about what the school library will become are essential for articulating the school library's future goals. Likewise, incorporating the Inquire, Collaborate, and Explore Shared Foundations when creating a school library vision embraces integrating background knowledge, coordinating learner groups, and questioning possible assumptions that affect the vision. The school librarians' guidebook, *National School Library Standards for Learners, School Librarians, and School Libraries,* is a roadmap to forming an effective plan for establishing a school library vision statement.

**NOTE**

1. https://www.ge.com/annual00/download/images/GEannual00.pdf

# Innovation

# 2

Innovation relates to strategic thinking, transformational change, and positive results by pushing and challenging ideas that are new and different. When authentically integrating technology into library instruction, school librarians as information specialists need to be informed about and willing to try new technologies for themselves to improve processes and products developed in the school library. Initiating new ideas related to the instructional plan and school library services means piloting and introducing programs and services that are untested. This aspect often causes the school librarian to become uncomfortable. Successful school librarians who plan strategically as program administrators know that innovative ideas are worth the risk because transformational change positions the school library for future success.

The first step in developing an innovative spirit is to be open to new ideas. Albert Einstein stated, "The world we have created is a product of our thinking; it cannot be changed without changing our thinking."[1] Dictionary.com defines *mindset* as "an attitude, disposition, or mood."[2] School librarians who are willing to change their thinking and attitudes have a growth mindset. A growth mindset is necessary for school librarians to embrace innovation. Carol Dweck researched and developed theories that relate to mindsets of learners. One of her conclusions was that growth mindset is more than effort; it is a willingness to learn and improve. She stated that learners need to "try new strategies and seek input from others when they're stuck" (Dweck 2015). School librarians who are innovative try new strategies and seek input from others before they reach an implementation roadblock.

## Options for Innovative Strategies

Finding and creating new initiatives depend on knowing how to expand instruction and services in the school library. The vision from chapter 1 is central to changing practices. The sample vision statement posits that *new and emerging resources that encourage collaboration and extend student learning will be evaluated, acquired, and equitably available to learners.* How this goal is accomplished can be routine or innovative. The school librarian who researches personal learning environments, social media, and vendor products discovers options based on developing technologies.

### *Personal Learning Environments*

Some examples of innovation are the introduction and integration of varied digital resources. Schools tap into personal learning environments that serve as a digital locker for learners. Their work is loaded onto these sites and shared with the classroom educator and the school librarian. School librarians use the survey option available on many personal learning platforms when seeking input from learners about a lesson or an assignment. Graphing of resulting information from the survey is often built into the learning platform and provides valuable data related to what worked in a lesson; more important, it provides insight into what did not work. Modifications to the instructional experience improve lessons. Often the personal learning platform provides a means for video chats and online meetings. A powerful collaboration tool that learners use in this digital community is the online meeting space. Many variations to the learners' experiences are possible when the school librarian chooses to incorporate new technology into the school library.

Some school librarians model innovative instruction by using the same technologies that learners use—for example, incorporating voice-activated devices into instruction as a novel introduction to finding information. Most educators come up with basic uses for a voice-activated device, such as reading a story or answering low-level questions. What might happen if a research project were launched by using a voice-activated device? What if the school librarian were to ask the device a question related to an inquiry-based curriculum project? Many of these devices are linked to apps that are research-based. The answer may lead learners to topics that widen or narrow their exploration. For example, asking a voice-activated device, "What are the causes of the American Civil War?" may elicit a response that includes *Uncle Tom's Cabin,* Bleeding Kansas, and slavery. Some devices share where the information originated, and some provide sources for further research. When an opinion question is posed, the voice-activated response may be, "Sorry, I don't know that." A lesson on fact or opinion is an appropriate spin-off from the responses because these devices answer with facts but not opinions (Davis 2018).

### Social Media

Encouraging learners to share their opinions and their work is a key component of the Shared Foundations. Sharing is accomplished when learners take pictures of their projects, tape their book review, or document makerspace projects and then post them to places learners visit online. School librarians use social media to promote programs, encourage student voice and innovation, and build a brand (Brown 2017).

An example of using new tools is the mobile app Flipgrid, recognized as one of the 2017 AASL Best Apps for Teaching and Learning. Flipgrid was developed by a team at the University of Minnesota and is suggested for all levels of learners. School librarians can "post topics in grids and students respond in video of prescribed lengths under three minutes. Responses now include transcripts and individual responses have their own hyperlinks" (AASL 2017).

Another source of new tools that connect learners to technology is the AASL Best Websites for Teaching and Learning. As of 2018, each app or website recognized in these lists is connected to the Shared Foundations through icons. School librarians attempting to use interactive websites that are trusted and evaluated and that support the new national standards need to make AASL's Best Apps and Websites for Teaching and Learning a first stop when planning lessons.

### Vendor Products

Library vendors continue to push forward with products to solve information management and learners' instructional needs. Information for databases scaffolds from elementary through high school to provide learners with a systematic progression from concrete and guided to conceptual and self-reliant information gathering. The databases are aligned with curriculum to provide relevance and context to topics. Vendors create pathways for learners to share, save, and download information, thereby expanding the learning environment. Innovative librarians explain to vendors what is needed to make instruction engaging and expansive. In turn, vendors use development teams to improve products that push the boundaries of learning forward.

## Solving Problems

Innovation solves problems and improves existing practices. Progress and change result when school librarians make conscious decisions about lesson design while expecting high-level outcomes. Innovation is resource-based, or process related. Every school librarian has opportunities to solve school-wide issues by creating programs that address academic needs in school improvement plans. A school improvement plan addresses such concerns as how to raise test scores, improve reading skills, reduce obesity in the school population, or even solve discipline issues. In each of these examples, school librarians become part of the solution when they adopt innovative strategies to solve school-wide issues. A district library supervisor worked with the district physical education specialist on a plan to place four stationary bikes in every secondary school library in the district. The creative and unique reading programs that evolved when the bikes became part of the school library solved literacy as well as physical fitness concerns. Learners who were unable to dress for physical education rode the bikes with the goal of meeting target heart rates, yet they were reading during the entire time. In one school, staff and students mapped out their travel across the country by riding and reading during study halls and planning periods. The bike program solved a problem in an innovative way because it drew learners into the school library while offering a unique literacy and fitness program.

## Constraints of Innovation

Being innovative is more than coming up with ideas; it is knowingly accepting the responsibilities associated with change. Successful school librarians "who encourage innovation are calculated risk takers. They minimize risk by segmenting a project and researching each part" (Martin 2013, 153). This research includes determining how a new concept for service fulfills the values of the school community's goals. School librarians who use questioning skills to evaluate the challenges and advantages of innovative ideas are politically astute. Working with others, the school librarian positions innovation so that stakeholders experience the wins. School librarians, as instructional partners, determine who benefits from change and seek input from these stakeholders by asking questions that engage their participation. Inviting administrators, other educators, and learners to share their perceptions about a new idea creates buy-in for projects. This team of stakeholders is a natural support system for the school librarian who is trying to implement a cutting-edge program.

Risk takers, apart from others in the school, have a good eye for the future, understand how to creatively solve problems, and are not afraid of failing. Having a good eye for the future means analyzing district and school goals to determine how the school library creatively engages learners, both educators and student learners, in the change. Risk takers see opportunities in problems and find solutions within the school library to solve them. School librarians who are risk takers view failure as a learning opportunity because when obstacles arise, librarians evaluate the causes and resulting effects that create barriers for instruction and learners. Through brainstorming solutions with the school library team and other stakeholders, school librarians make adjustments that will move the project forward. The risk-taking process inspires and motivates relevant, engaged school librarians.

## Connecting to the Shared Foundations

Improvement and change come when school librarians make conscious decisions about innovation in the library. High-level improvements are the result of reducing risk by strategically introducing change. The structures for building skills identified with strategic thinking are in the Frameworks for School Librarians and School Libraries within the Think Domain and are specifically associated with the Shared Foundations of Inquire, Collaborate, and Explore. Applying the principles from the AASL Standards both within and outside the school library space will amplify the school librarian's success in accomplishing innovative change in the library.

### INQUIRE

In the Shared Foundation of Inquire in the Domain Think, one of the School Librarian Competencies is "encouraging learners to formulate questions about a personal interest or a curricular topic" (AASL 2018a, 47). In order to be innovative, school librarians need to push for the formulation not just of basic questions but of higher order thinking questions that cannot be answered with a simple yes or no. Jeffrey Wilhelm, professor of education at Boise State University, explained the purpose and gave examples of essential questions in his *Knowledge Quest* article, "Learning to Love the Questions." He stated, "We further know that creativity and innovation involve questioning and the capacity to frame topics as problems to be solved" (Wilhelm 2014, 37). These questions need to be grounded in authentic language and have real-life connections for learners in order for learners to want to take the time and energy to answer them. School librarians need to create opportunities, both formal and informal, for themselves, learners, and fellow educators to formulate questions.

There are varied examples of how school librarians can create formal opportunities for learners to formulate questions. The formal opportunities show a conscious decision by the school librarian to cultivate a learning environment that values questioning for both process and product purposes. One example is the modeling of asking questions and seeking answers in the school library by designing a question specifically to introduce the lesson. As an instructional partner, the school librarian can facilitate this modeling for educators when collaborating on an instructional lesson. The question may be about the theme of a book to be read during that lesson.

It may be about how a social studies historical event or person affects the learner's current life. It could be about how researching a science topic of choice affects the learner's lifestyle decisions later. These specifically designed questions help to keep the lesson focused while modeling how the question-and-answer process works.

During formal instruction, it is crucial for the school librarian to allow for deliberate reflective time during lessons for learners to write down questions. This time that is intentionally set aside could be included in the formative or summative assessments, or in both. The questions could be a reaction to what the learner discovered during the research process or may be developed ahead of time for consideration later. Whether questions are shared among the learners and educators involved in the lesson or are kept for personal reflection will depend on the school librarian's assessment of the situation and the overall instructional plan.

Asking learners to create book reviews is another formal opportunity for school librarians to develop higher level questioning and thinking. Writing book reviews facilitates both the development of critical reading skills and the emergence of a voice about how and why people like or don't like what they read. Writing book reviews includes internal higher level questioning for the learners to process and share what they read. In addition to facilitating the new format of critiquing read material and learning to articulate story elements, the school librarian as information specialist can be innovative by introducing new technology to develop and share book reviews. One of the Inquire best practices involves encouraging "learners to consider a variety of products to use as they demonstrate their learning" (AASL 2018a, 74).

Informal opportunities for school librarians to reinforce formulating questions occur daily in the school library. Whether the learner (or educator) is using the space and available resources to find information for a personal interest or an assignment, the interactions between the learner and the school librarian allow for the chance to advance questioning skills. Taking advantage of informal opportunities promotes the school library as an environment of authentic questioning while reinforcing the disposition of inquiry as an effective way to learn.

One example of an informal opportunity is having conversations with learners about their learning choices, focusing on why they chose a particular topic or resource. Discussing the quality of a resource with a fellow educator fosters communication and respect. When school librarians show genuine interest in a learner's work by asking questions, learners become more comfortable sharing their ideas and opinions. Another example of an informal opportunity is using a question prompt to get learners started on writing blog posts or tweets about what they learned in the school library or what they recently read. These informal opportunities provide as much higher level questioning and thought as do formal opportunities while building relationships.

The formal and informal opportunities created by school librarians are put into action through the school library when enabling "curiosity and initiative by embedding the inquiry process within grade bands and within disciplines" (AASL 2018a, School Library I.A.1.). "Learners are self-directed and life-spanning" (AASL 2018a, 10) and can include both young and older stakeholders. School librarians, through the interconnected five roles of leader, instructional partner, information specialist, teacher, and program administrator, know that all stakeholders in the school library can benefit from the inquiry process to maximize personal and professional learning.

## COLLABORATE

In the Shared Foundation Collaborate, "scaffolding enactment of learning-group roles to enable the development of new understandings within a group" is an invitation for school librarians to show innovation (AASL 2018a, School Librarian III.A.2.). The IRIS Center at Vanderbilt University's Peabody College defines *instructional scaffolding* as "a process through which a teacher adds supports for students in order to enhance learning and aid in the mastery of tasks. . . . As students master the assigned tasks, the supports are gradually removed" (IRIS Center 2018). Instructional scaffolding can be applied when the school librarian provides support for setting the role expectation when people work together in groups. Once the learners recognize their role in the overall group and how it affects the success of the group, the school librarian allows the group complete independence on meeting its goals. As learners move through an instructional task, they may decide to redefine the roles initially provided by the school librarian. Using scaffolding for instruction is innovative when the school librarian fosters a climate in which it is acceptable for learners' mindsets to change as gathering information creates new insight into the instructional project. Not only is it innovative for a school librarian to allow learners to modify their group roles as instruction progresses and changes, but scaffolding also empowers learners by giving them control of the instructional process.

The positive results of scaffolding can also impact educators when it is used as a tool in professional development sessions hosted by the school library and led by the school librarian. "The school library facilitates opportunities to integrate collaborative and shared learning by partnering with other educators to scaffold learning and organize learner groups to broaden and deepen understanding" (AASL 2018a, School Library III.A.1.). In these professional development sessions, the educators become the learners who benefit from being organized to interact with and realize the potential of innovative information resources and technology in their classroom environments. As instructional partner, the school librarian collaborates with the technology specialists in the building or at the district level to implement the professional development goals. The school librarian, as information specialist and teacher, empowers the building educators to ask questions and make effective decisions, integrating their newly acquired knowledge to impact instruction.

## EXPLORE

"Encouraging learners to read widely and deeply in multiple formats and write and create for a variety of purposes" leads to innovation and transformational change in many ways (AASL 2018a, School Librarian V.A.1.). School librarians with the disposition to model and support opportunities to read, write, and create bring about positive change in learners' attitudes about the school library and learning. This positive change happens when the school librarian makes purposeful collection development decisions and effective instructional decisions.

The collection development aspect of the school library is crucial to the construction of an effective physical and virtual presence within the larger school community. The selected print and digital resources determine how the physical space of the school library is arranged in order for learners to access and effectively use the resources. As program administrators, "school librarians conduct ongoing reviews of the school library's collection, technology, and management policies and update them to ensure that new and emerging resource formats and the needs of diverse learning populations are addressed" (AASL 2018a, 171). Resources can include updated devices and apps for equitable use by learners and educators as well as notebooks that stay in the school library for writing and creative enrichment opportunities, depending on the developmental needs of the learners. The choice of fiction and nonfiction reading materials in multiple formats establishes and promotes the expectation of reading for personal and academic growth among all stakeholders.

The instructional decisions made by the school librarian can be seen in both structured or unstructured opportunities. Structured opportunities include formal instructional lessons, reading promotions, and research times. These structured opportunities can be facilitated solely by the school librarian or in collaboration with the classroom educator as an instructional partner. The unstructured times may include providing learners with makerspaces and 3-D manipulatives to visualize their ideas and giving them free time and room in the school library space to process thoughts about an assigned or a personal topic.

The collection development and instructional decisions also impact the school library's innovation as a whole. "The school library supports learners' personal curiosity by providing resources and strategies for inquiry-based processes" (AASL 2018a, School Library V.A.1.). The results of inquiry-based processes are maximized to foster innovation when the resources and strategies to effectively apply them are intentionally purchased and shared. Stakeholders are excited and motivated to become more invested when the school library encourages their personal curiosity with its allocation of resources and physical space capabilities.

## Stimulating Innovation

Innovation depends on the school librarian's knowledge about how to use resources available to expand instruction and services in the library. The school librarian who explores digital options, such as personal learning environments, social media, and vendor products, stimulates innovation based on developing technologies. As personal learning environments continue to become more accessible from a cost and implementation standpoint, the school library's instructional program is enriched. School librarians can use personal learning components to identify learners' goals and link to social networks. More important, school librarians develop digital learning spaces and experiences that address learners' needs. Social media offer another stimulus for student learning because they increase student engagement and provide both sharing and communication skills. School librarians working as program administrators develop rapport with vendors by explaining their individual learners' needs as new products are developed. In addition, school librarians can help vendors meet the learners needs by reviewing products and making suggestions for improvements.

Innovation is achieved in various ways by the school librarian who is willing to strive for transformational change while accepting anticipated risks. Any new idea, technology, or process will meet with resistance as implementation begins. The school librarian is an information specialist who understands the school community and positions new technologies to solve academic and access problems. If done authentically to benefit learners' development of literacy skills and instructional experiences, the outcomes of innovation outweigh the risks. Innovation is evident when school librarians incorporate the skills outlined in the Competencies and Alignments in the Think Domain of the AASL Standards Frameworks for School Librarians and School Libraries in the Shared Foundations of Inquire, Collaborate, and Explore. Integrating new emerging technologies, designing a solid collection of digital and print resources, and encouraging stakeholders to amplify what they have learned in the school library lead to positive change. The positive change starts with the individual stakeholder but spreads to the larger school community.

### NOTES

1. https://izquotes.com/quote/301799
2. www.dictionary.com/browse/mindset

# 3

# Initiative

In the book entitled *The Ersatz Elevator,* Lemony Snicket says, "If we wait until we're ready, we'll be waiting for the rest of our lives. Let's go" (*Deseret News* 2015). Initiators counteract complacency in the school environment with actions. School librarians who are initiators use an idea to revitalize one or more aspects of the library, then act. Their actions create energy when they use ingenuity to assess the current school library resources and services, then initiate change.

Taking initiative affects transformational change by creating the spark that launches innovative services to bring positive results to the school library. Outcomes that realign the school library to push the program toward the future indicate how and why it is important to take action and follow through with ideas. Initiative is not only what you do but how you do it. What you do may relate to ideas, programs, services, or implementation of standards. How you do it might be better characterized as, "Why wait?" When school librarians create vision that guides innovation, they must then take initiative to start transformational change. With innovation comes a realignment in ideas, policies, and decisions made in the school library. The resulting progress is evident in the professional growth of the school librarian and ultimately through the learners' success in the school library.

## Pursuing Collaborative Opportunities

School librarians act on ideas in various ways. As they perform each of the five roles of leader, instructional partner, information specialist, teacher, and program administrator, innovative ideas are implemented to meet school library objectives. In addition, there are collaborative opportunities with different stakeholders in the building and at the district level. These stakeholders include learners, fellow educators, administrators, and community members. School librarians show initiative by considering every opportunity as an opening to better the school library. For example, school librarians work to integrate technology into the school library, connect to district goals, strive to be a member of the school leadership team, and realize that new ideas create new possibilities for expanding the school library's sphere of influence. Utilizing collaborative opportunities enhances student instruction and serves as a model for learners.

## Integration of Technology

Authentic integration of technology can be seen in the following example: an elementary school librarian witnessed a shift in her second graders' learning when she chose to collaborate with her instructional technology resource teacher (ITRT) to select an app that would make creating stories, both the writing and illustration aspects, more interactive. The ITRT taught the school librarian how to set up the Book Creator application for use with each class and model the creation process with her learners. The second graders thrived when they used the program, and it enhanced their writing and illustration skills. The learners also appreciated being able to showcase what they had developed with their peers (Roberts 2018).

## Support for District Goals

Another way to take action is to pay attention to school and district initiatives and figure out how the school library can support those initiatives—for example, by becoming involved in a PTA-developed and -sponsored International Night at the school level. When the school librarian in the roles of information specialist and instructional partner reaches out to classroom educators to collaborate on research projects about different continents, the learners make a connection to the topic being researched. This connection is due to co-planning whereby the school librarian challenges "learners to reflect and question assumptions and possible misconceptions" related to the cultures represented by learners in the school (AASL 2018a, School Librarian V.A.2.). Ultimately, learners participate and make an investment in the success of the event because their work becomes the focal point of the International Night. Displays featuring learners' research provide information about countries of the world and the contributions of different cultures to the world, our country, their school, and learners' individual lives. District-level initiatives require school librarians to take a broader view of their instruction and how it affects the larger demographic of the district. Working with colleagues across schools gives the district consistency in the skills being taught in the school libraries.

### Membership on the School Leadership Team

A school librarian's membership on the school leadership team provides valuable access to school-wide data and instructional needs. Realizing the specific aspect of student learning that the school is focused on dictates instructional decisions throughout the school year. A building-level school librarian realized that she could meet the need to achieve individual student growth by increasing reading vocabulary scores, which was a goal in the continuous school improvement plan. The intent was to use vocabulary scores from the Northwest Evaluation Association's Measurement of Academic Progress assessment tool. Selecting primarily picture books to give the learners authentic examples of the more abstract vocabulary terms (for example, *satire, irony*) helped the terms to stick. Over the course of four years, the percentage of third graders who met or exceeded goals in learning the vocabulary terms went from 44 percent to 76 percent, which benefited everyone involved in the learning process (Roberts 2018).

### Promotion of New Ideas

Though new ideas create opportunities for school librarians to show initiative, sometimes a policy review and adjustment creates a more stable learning environment. Knowledgeable school librarians who are leaders and program administrators keep up to date on trends both locally and nationally and then use new information to examine the school library's current policies. This approach takes initiative to delve into an area that others may be more comfortable leaving alone. For example, a district supervisor of school libraries initiated a change to the instructional materials review policy in response to a book challenge. A challenge regarding sexual content in the book *Snow Falling on Cedars* by David Guterson went through the review process, and the book was retained by the committee and the school board. Then a comment was made that the book needed to be brought back under review because of profanity. The district-level library supervisor wondered if a book just reviewed could be immediately challenged again. Would the second challenge be considered double jeopardy? Nothing in the instructional materials review policy addressed how often a book could be challenged. After studying the issue and receiving information from the American Library Association's Office of Intellectual Freedom, the district supervisor initiated action to adjust the school board's policy to accommodate changes in social mores. This policy change would be in place whether the committee decided to retain or remove the title. The result was the following addition to the policy: "The School Board action pertaining to the Instructional Materials Review Committee recommendation will remain in effect for a period of four (4) years. After this time the material may be reconsidered following selection policy guidelines" (HCPS 2012). This change enabled the school librarians to bring back a book by reconsidering it based on selection policy guidelines. It also stabilized activity surrounding multiple challenges of the same book.

## Taking Action

Decisions generate opportunities for school librarians to show initiative. Nike's Just Do It campaign was the product of a thoughtful decision to expand the brand in a way that would inspire and energize not only customers but also the internal culture of the company (Conlon 2015). As with the Nike results, school librarians are energized and inspired by making decisions to implement change in the school library. In examining how Nike came up with the Just Do It concept, it is evident that research and reflection were embedded into the process that led to a final decision. School librarians must research and reflect on new ideas, but the essential component to accomplishing change is the decision to act. That is initiative.

## Overcoming Barriers

Initiative is a leadership challenge for school librarians when there is tension between being ready and acting. Just as ideas, policies, and decisions create opportunities for change, they may create barriers for school librarians. Ideas remain abstract until someone connects them with a need. Often the school community views new ideas as unreasonable for a multitude of reasons. School librarians must show initiative by educating stakeholders about the necessity and resulting successes of a change. Written and unwritten procedures and policies can be restrictive for the school librarian who shows initiative. It is important for the school librarian to follow set guidelines and use them not to restrict but as a vehicle for moving ideas forward. Sometimes school and district decisions create priorities that impede school library change by preventing resources of time, funding, and personnel to be directed toward new school library services. All these environmental conditions challenge school librarians to think creatively, seek collaboration, and solve problems.

## Connecting to the Shared Foundations

AASL serves as a model initiator by continuously looking toward the future and revising standards for school librarians and school libraries. As early as 1925, standards described what services elementary and secondary school libraries should provide. From that point forward, ALA and AASL have systematically surveyed the educational environment and released new standards that reflect trends in the school community while giving a fresh perspective for transforming learning going forward (AASL 2018a, 4–7). Taking initiative needs to be based on solid ideas to be successful. The Think Domain in the Shared Foundations of Inquire, Collaborate, and Explore in the AASL Standards Frameworks for School Librarians and School Libraries cultivates the thinking needed before taking initiative.

## INQUIRE

"School librarians teach learners to display curiosity and initiative when seeking information by encouraging learners to formulate questions about a personal interest or a curricular topic" (AASL 2018a, School Librarian I.A.1.). For the school librarian, the question becomes how best to model for learners how to take initiative by following the inquiry-based process. Makerspaces provide an effective way to display curiosity and initiative. Using 3-D manipulatives results in success because they allow learners to fail and then improve their project. Through hands-on interactive materials, learners are challenged to make their ideas and proposed visualizations real. When school librarians create opportunities for learners to ask higher level questions during research and about personal topics, the research process flourishes. The learning is personalized, and life connections are made. As learners realize that school library resources satisfy curiosity and help find answers, their buy-in to the school library increases. Understanding how to access and use the resources through instruction makes the investment stronger.

School librarians also realize the importance of modeling the inquiry-based process for other educators. The role of instructional partner is vital to the school librarian because it forms connections with other educators both in the same building and at the district level. "The school library enables curiosity and initiative by using a systematic instructional-development and information-search process in working with other educators to improve integration of the process into curriculum" (AASL 2018a, School Library I.A.2.). At the school building level, this modeling can be seen through professional development sessions offered after school for faculty or collaboration on an authentic, curriculum-based lesson with school library resources and the inquiry process firmly embedded into the experience.

At the district level, this modeling can take the form of inquiry-based process discussions held at quarterly meetings about current issues or small groups to receive feedback about possible lesson ideas.

## COLLABORATE

To collaborate with another person for the purpose of attaining goals is a powerful experience. Whether they are playing on the same team or working together on a project, learners realize the benefits of taking initiative to work with other people to develop skills that attain success. "School librarians facilitate collaborative opportunities by challenging learners to work with others to broaden and deepen understandings" (AASL 2018a, School Librarian III.A.1.). Knowing that collaboration is an effective learning tool for creating richer experiences, school librarians can take several different paths to facilitate collaborative opportunities for learners. One path is to model collaboration with classroom educators. Seeing collaboration in action empowers learners to follow suit in their own learning. They are able to witness how each individual brings skill sets and expertise to the process and product. "Showing administrators and the broader school community a collaboration rubric that shows how you collaborated with educators can help tell the story of exactly how you and the school library impact learning" (AASL 2018a, 91).

Another path is for school librarians to create learner groups and activities within the school library that foster collaboration. The groups can be organized for problem-based learning or for using science, technology, engineering, and mathematics (STEM) manipulatives to create solutions to real-life problems. One Collaborate best practice is to "ensure that each group includes a mix of talents, experiences, learning styles, and ideas when grouping learners. Members of mixed-aptitude groups often learn more from one another than members of groups in which all learners have the same skills and ideas" (AASL 2018a, 91). Although it can be challenging to participate in these learner groups, the results of the collaboration show learners the power and benefit of working together to solve problems.

Developing a culture of collaboration brings more stakeholders in the school community together and creates a larger opportunity for academic success. As the program administrator and leader of the school library, the school librarian realizes this ideal. "The school library facilitates opportunities to integrate collaborative and shared learning by leading inquiry-based learning opportunities that enhance the information, media, visual, and technical literacies of all members of the school community" (AASL 2018a, School Library III.A.2.). When the school librarian seizes the opportunity to create welcoming and resource-rich virtual and physical spaces, stakeholders are encouraged to take the initiative to enhance their own literacies. The virtual space has to be well organized, be easily accessible, and contain developmentally appropriate resources for stakeholders. The physical space needs to be arranged for different activities to occur simultaneously while promoting independence. Making stakeholders aware of these decisions about how to allocate resources shows the initiative taken by the school librarian.

## EXPLORE

Exploration in the school library includes both mental and physical exploration. "School librarians foster learners' personal curiosity by enabling learners by helping them develop inquiry-based processes for personal growth" (AASL 2018a, School Librarian V.A.3.). Stakeholders take initiative when searching for personal growth topics of choice. School librarians foster mental exploration by building a strong collection, including print and digital resources, which ensures that stakeholders have the opportunity to ask questions and find quality answers. One example of a valuable print resource for mental exploration is the picture book series What Do You Do With . . . ?, written by Kobi Yamada. These stories contain examples of communicating the exciting and scary parts of a problem, an idea, or a chance. Learners can relate to the main character who is trying to realize how embracing one of these opportunities affects a life. School librarians and classroom educators at all levels can use this resource as a prompt for initiative and personal growth by having learners focus on a chosen problem, idea, or chance that can be supported by the school library resources.

"The school library supports learners' personal curiosity by fostering opportunities for learners to demonstrate personal curiosity and creation of knowledge through engaging with a wide variety of resources and technology" (AASL 2018a, School Library V.A.2.). Physical exploration of resources and technology is encouraged when the school library is arranged in an organized plan with areas designated for different purposes. The well-thought-out space, with areas for reading, research, collaborative projects, and 3-D STEM manipulatives, respects the connection between learners' need to take initiative in their personal learning and the school library's role in encouraging personal growth. When the learners' needs are met, learners are empowered to take authentic action in their own learning.

## Taking the First Step

Begin, start, kick off, initiate the school librarian's vision for innovation. Showing initiative is the first step leaders make because it creates energy for the school library by sparking a shift in services or philosophy. It ignites transformational change that culminates from decisions guided by strategic thinking. Initiative is a disposition and skill that act to implement the ideas in a vision. Sometimes initiative is the simple act of helping a learner in need, while at other times, initiative fulfills groundbreaking ideas. The future of the school library requires leadership from school librarians to initiate ideas, programs, services, policies, and standards in the educational environment. Technology integration requires initiative to explore the infrastructure, hardware, and software that provide reliable access for learners and educators. Initiative involves paying attention to building-level and district initiatives and deciding how the school library can support them. Seeking membership on the school leadership team is critical for knowing and understanding the academic objectives being driven by administration. Building on ideas from the leadership team, educators, and learners and then taking action facilitate positive change for the school library. School librarians deepen their resolve to take initiative by experiencing and reflecting on the Competencies for the School Librarian and the Alignments for the School Library found in the Shared Foundations of Inquire, Collaborate, and Explore in the Think Domain. This growth mindset is strengthened because the reason for change is clarified by the standards. In addition, the Shared Foundations create leverage to support the outcomes that school librarians intend. A school librarian displays initiative by accepting Leonardo da Vinci's challenge: "Being willing is not enough; we must do."[1]

**NOTE**

1. https://www.brainyquote.com/quotes/leonardo_da_vinci_120052

## Reflection Questions

Provide thoughtful answers to the following reflection questions using the lines provided.

What is your vision for your school library?

_____

_____

What specific innovations do you have in mind to expand your library services?

_____

_____

How will you initiate change with the educators and learners in your school environment?

_____

_____

How are vision, innovation, and taking initiative interrelated to support strategic thinking?

_____

_____

What other Shared Foundations, Domains, and Competencies and Alignments in the AASL Standards Frameworks for School Librarians and School Libraries could you apply to strategic thinking through vision, innovation, and taking initiative? Explain how you could apply them.

_____

_____

PART A: STRATEGIC THINKING

## Self-Assessment

**Goal:** To self-assess my objectives and take action for strategic thinking for the school library

| My Tasks | I will not be ready to focus on this until next school year. | I want to focus on this within the next three months. | Possible next steps (key collaborators, resources needed, policy requirements) |
|---|---|---|---|
| **To decide whether a new vision statement needs to be written for the school library** | | | |
| **To list specific Common Beliefs that a new vision will incorporate** | | | |
| **To write down prior knowledge that affects a new vision** | | | |
| **To write down which current assumptions are being challenged by a new vision** | | | |
| **To initiate an innovative program or service** | | | |
| **To identify potential roadblocks to transformational changes** | | | |
| **To identify which learners will support innovation and change** | | | |

## Breakthrough Skills

Based on the chapters in this section on strategic thinking, there are three professional growth breakthroughs to focus on and strengthen. These breakthroughs are questioning skills, working with groups, and accepting risks. To assist with growth in these areas, use the Competency Assessment Cycle of Design, Enact, Adjust, and Reflect from AASL's *National School Library Standards* (figure A.1):

- **Design:** Recognize an opportunity and plan to change.

- **Enact:** Test the change by studying where you are to gather baseline information.

- **Adjust:** Review and enact an improvement activity and analyze the results to determine what you learned.

- **Reflect:** Document what you learned, reflect on whether changes need to be made, then, after adjustments, repeat the process (AASL 2018a, 126–127).

----

**FIGURE A.1**

## Competency assessment cycle

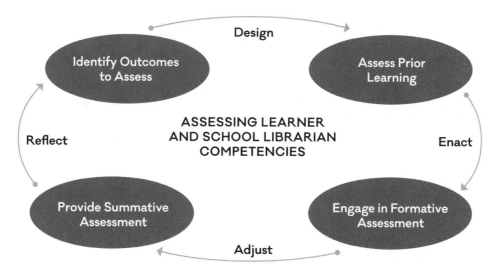

Source: From the AASL *National School Library Standards for Learners, School Librarians, and School Libraries,* p. 126, standards.aasl.org, © 2018 American Library Association.

The competency assessment model is designed to provide continuous improvement. As school librarians, we are committed to lifelong learning, which is continuous knowledge growth to improve ourselves and our practice.

## Attaining Growth through Assessing Competencies

| Areas to Assess | Design | Enact | Adjust | Reflect |
|---|---|---|---|---|
| **Questioning Skills** | Realize and identify higher level questioning outcomes to benefit instruction. | Tape yourself teaching to determine what level of questions you pose to students. | Review the tape and categorize the level of each question asked to determine impact on instruction. | Revise and redesign each question to elevate it to a higher level of thinking. |
| **Working with Groups** | Formulate objectives for the group based on a specific library goal. | Gather an ideal stakeholder group and meet to solve problems for a specific library project. | Organize group suggestions and ideas. Revise the original goal if needed. Implement the goal. | Check the results of the goal for what went well and what needs improvement. Make changes and relaunch. |
| **Accepting Risks** | Engage in inquiry-based processes to determine risk factors. | Gather data from stakeholders to determine needs related to library services. | Review data to analyze assumptions and possible misconceptions of stakeholders. | Create buy-in by connecting the library service to stakeholder concerns and launch the project. |

# Decision Making

At the core of every action is a decision. When decisions are well thought out, the resulting response creates answers to a need. Decisions that are intuitive and reactionary resolve questions as well. Reactionary decisions can be beneficial if they are the result of higher order thinking that originates from practicing a process of sound decision making. This section presents a practical blueprint for decision making. Decision making is directly related to problem solving, critical thinking, and emotional resilience. Modeling the decision-making skills of problem solving and critical thinking ensures multiple pathways to informed, thoughtful results for school librarians and their stakeholders. This modeling can be seen through collaboration with classroom educators as an instructional partner. It can also be seen when school librarians express and share their own frustration and perseverance during the research process and choice of reading material. Central to decision making is fostering a culture of emotional resilience whereby learners and school librarians become more flexible in their opinions and decisions during changing circumstances. Integrating problem solving, critical thinking, and emotional resilience skills into the decision-making process creates a high level of professional mastery.

## A Decision-Making Challenge for School Librarians

An overarching decision-making problem that school librarians face in their work is the learners' need for a quick answer. The instant gratification that learners experience from living in a fast-paced digital environment stifles their emotional resilience to keep researching when answers are not immediately evident. For example, during the research process, learners expect that the information they want will be explicitly stated in their first resource choice. When this is not the case, learners then tend to type the topic in the browser search bar and hope for better source choices. Also, learners choose material for pleasure reading and then read only a small amount before returning the material. They don't realize that giving time and energy to reading choices usually increases the amount of satisfaction received from the material. By identifying situations that offer opportunities for the development of decision-making skills, school librarians are proactively facilitating authentic connections that will assist learners in applying the learned skills outside school. The Domain Create is important for learners and school librarians because it stresses developing their existing knowledge and creating new knowledge. The AASL Standards Frameworks for School Librarians and School Libraries provide an opportunity for school librarians to practice the Competencies and Alignments from the Shared Foundations of Inquire, Curate, and Explore. Inquire promotes questioning and curiosity, both of which are necessary for learners to overcome the need for quick answers. Curate encourages learners to complete deep inquiry through reflection. And Explore stresses fostering a growth mindset.

# 4

# Problem Solving

W ith the influx of video games, tried-and-true board games do not get a lot of playing time. The parents of two boys ages 13 and 15 decided that breaks from the teens' various electronic devices were important. One solution the parents provided was the board game Parcheesi. Parcheesi is a game for two to four players whose pawns race around a board. The goal is for each player to move his pawns from the starting position to the home square. To do this, the pawns must complete a loop around the board. The winner is the first player to move all four of his pawns around the board and land on the home square. The design of Parcheesi encourages making decisions. Pawns move based on a roll of two dice, so some of the game relies on probability. Players may bump opponents' pawns, sending the pawns back to the start, and they can create a blockade, which prevents any pawn from moving forward. "So, it's not all just a roll of the dice; Parcheesi is set up so that every move involves important strategic questions. Do I use the combined or individual numbers on the dice? Which pawn do I move? What are my priorities— safety, blockading, or bumping another player?" (Wachtel 2012). To answer any of these questions requires what is termed the "[cycle] of design, implementation, and reflection" (figure 4.1; AASL 2018a, 51). Breaking this cycle down into action steps forms a problem-solving process to practice. Whether it is intentional or not, the parents of these boys are increasing their sons' problem-solving stamina by providing an opportunity to think through strategies that will win the game.

## The Problem-Solving Process

Just as Parcheesi requires players to problem solve, school librarians faced with making a decision should practice specific steps to problem solve. A four-step problem-solving

**FIGURE 4.1**

## The cycle of design, implementation, and reflection

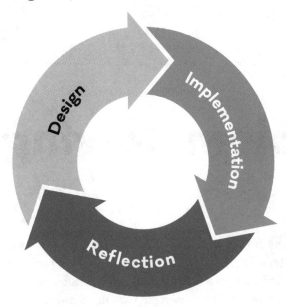

process that school librarians can master is to identify the problem, gather data, implement a solution, then evaluate and reflect on the results. There may be other methods, but the important thing is that school librarians practice and use a strategy for systematic problem solving.

### Step 1: Identify the Problem

Much like players of a board game, school librarians may sense that there are numbers of questions bombarding them when problems arise. Sometimes these questions obscure the actual problem. As program administrator, the school librarian realizes that identifying the real problem is not always easy or direct and requires a careful, well-thought-out process to recognize the need within the questions. In other instances, the questions come from results of the problem. For example, when a school librarian with limited funds is choosing which resources to select for the library, is lack of budget the problem or is the allocation of funds (a result of the budget) the real complication? If needing a larger budget is the problem, then a solution would be to brainstorm monetary resources to provide additional funding. If the allocation of funding is the problem, then realigning the dollars to match the need is necessary. The best problem-solving results occur when the school librarian clearly pinpoints the issue to be solved.

**FIGURE 4.2**

## Problem-solving Ishikawa or Fishbone Diagram

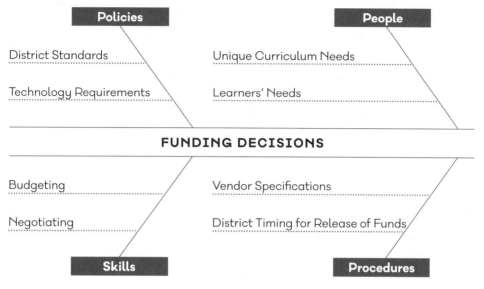

**Policies**

District Standards

Technology Requirements

**People**

Unique Curriculum Needs

Learners' Needs

**FUNDING DECISIONS**

Budgeting

Negotiating

Vendor Specifications

District Timing for Release of Funds

**Skills**

**Procedures**

## *Step 2: Gather Data*

Once the problem is identified, then the school librarian needs to gather data. Fortunately, many tools are available for collecting information when a problem emerges. Creating surveys by using online forms is one option for collecting data. Many free options are available online and allow survey designers to ask open-ended questions, multiple-choice questions via drop-down menus, or questions that use branching and logic. The submitted information can then be organized or graphed. Another method of gathering data is to form focus groups and give participants an opportunity to discuss a problem and brainstorm solutions.

An outgrowth of a small-group discussion may be graphing the information into a cause-and-effect diagram such as the Fishbone (Ishikawa) Diagram. When using the Fishbone Diagram, the school librarian as leader must decide what problem needs to be solved (ASQ 2018). Next, the group of stakeholders brainstorms issues from four major categories to identify underlying causes impacting the decision. In the school environment, often policies, people, skills, and procedures influence how decisions are made. When problem solving how a school librarian can best allocate limited funds, note that figure 4.2 provides four categories of possible causes that need review to determine if and how they affect budgeting. Some of the issues impacting funding allocation are listed under each of the four categories of policies, people, skills, and procedures. For example, policies related to *district standards* and *technology requirements* may change purchasing decisions. *Unique curriculum needs* may create demand for expensive materials that target a limited number of learners. Perhaps *learners' needs* for leveled materials impact the quantity of resources the school librarian can purchase. To stretch funds, the school librarian as program administrator must be trained to effectively *budget* based on need and optimum use. *Negotiating* skills are important when determining what will be funded as well as working to obtain the best price. *Vendor* deadlines and product enhancements may help or hinder purchases. And the *timing of the release of district funding* may complicate purchasing resources so they may be installed or cataloged for learners' use. Once these causes and their effects are discussed, the resulting information will point the school librarian toward purchases that are user driven.

### Step 3: Implement the Solution

After gathering data, the next step is to decide on a strategy that addresses the problem of funding. The school librarian is fulfilling the leader role when deciding on the most efficient strategy to address the problem. When purchasing materials to support the curriculum, learners, and library services, the strategy may be to focus on resources that correlate with the school improvement plan, support a curriculum need, or fill a gap in existing resources. Based on reliable data and user input, the solution to the problem is developed and implemented. Additional data are gathered as the resources are purchased and incorporated into library services. Referring to the Fishbone Diagram that identifies cause and effect, the school librarian uses the four causal categories and related issues when gathering data to determine the effectiveness of the purchases.

### Step 4: Evaluate and Reflect on the Results

To complete the problem-solving process, after collecting data, the school librarian reflects on the process and evaluates the effectiveness of the decisions. If changes need to be made in the future, then recommendations are drafted and projections are changed to more effectively fund school library resources. The evaluation completes the "cycle of design, implementation, and reflection" (AASL 2018a, 51).

## Data-Driven Versus Emotional Decisions

Problem solving is a necessary skill to teach to learners. The need for quick answers to questions hinders locating information supported by reliable data. When research is suspended before a topic is fully vetted, the learner's final product is compromised. School librarians who systematically work with stakeholders to make the process of problem solving a habit create learners who develop thoughtful conclusions based on strong data. Intentionally teaching the decision-making skills of problem solving when collaborating with classroom educators ensures multiple pathways to informed, thoughtful results for school librarians and their learners.

School librarians receive requests multiple times a day, from a learner needing a specific resource to a classroom teacher requesting time in the school library. Acknowledging that time constraints sometimes demand immediate decisions, it is extremely important that school librarians practice thoughtful thinking and planning before acting. Just as learners must use the problem-solving process to form accurate conclusions, school librarians know that each decision, no matter how large or small, requires strategies for positive problem solving. Otherwise, school librarians' decisions may flow from inconsistent and flawed reactions to larger situations.

For example, decision makers typically fall into several categories when solving problems. Some people make emotional decisions, some make quick decisions, and other people use data to drive their decisions. The research conclusions of Jennifer Lerner, a professor of public policy and management at Harvard, indicate that trusting gut feelings might be the wrong way to go about solving problems. Lerner's research delved into whether a happy mood, sad feelings, or even anger created sound decisions. Lerner found that decision makers in a happy mood put more faith in the length of the message than in the quality of the information. Problem solvers in a sad mood became impatient and made poor decisions. Lerner found that anger simplifies thinking by narrowing the causes so that all aspects of a problem are *not* considered. Emotions do play a part in problem solving, however, and school librarians need to acknowledge that emotions exist and then try not to let emotions totally control their decisions (Khazan 2016). Very much like an emotional decision maker, the problem solver who reacts quickly often creates solutions that lack data and critical thinking. Those who react without considering all the alternatives impacting the problem do not take into consideration long-term results. A momentary solution that is not well-thought-out can cause difficulties in the future. For example, allowing an educator to bring a class to the school library for research when the library is already at capacity creates a less than ideal experience for learners. The school library resources, both personnel and materials, may not be adequate to provide what learners need. In addition, the situation sets up learners and their classroom teacher for failure. The best decisions are made when data are incorporated to ensure that all aspects of a situation are considered. Data-driven decision makers identify the problem, gather data, implement a solution, and evaluate the results. School librarians in a leadership role know that effective decision making requires thinking and planning to get the full value of data gathering before finalizing program administration findings.

## Situational Awareness

Other considerations when problem solving are the concepts of awareness and assessment as they relate to problem solving. The military is best known for using situational awareness when relating to internal perception of the environment. Just as the military deals with environments that can change, when vetting information the school librarian needs to frequently monitor and clarify the current state of circumstances in the school before making a decision (Wellens 1993). This means being aware of the school's power brokers and how they impact the decision-making process. It means understanding the stakeholders who will be impacted by any decision made and focusing on their individual and group needs. The difficult part of situational awareness is that it is constantly changing, requiring the school librarian to shift attention from one solution to a variation of that solution when changes occur. Constant change also requires that the school librarian make a global scan of the school environment or focus on a specific department or assess a category of learners before making decisions. As an example, a district supervisor knew that one of the high schools in the district needed a large infusion of funds to boost the collection and make it relevant for learners. The supervisor visited an incoming administrator who was a school library supporter and requested funding for the school library collection based on the solid guidelines found in the district collection policy (AASL 2018a, School Library IV.B.3.). The principal immediately gave the school librarians $2,000 for new materials and promised to continue funding each year going forward. The district supervisor not only was aware of the principal's support for school libraries but also understood that timing was critical to receiving help. Once every department, club, and need were brought to the newly appointed administrator, it would be more difficult to obtain funds for the school library. This was a savvy, time-sensitive move on the part of the school library supervisor, whose situational awareness skills solved a problem by knowing when and how to approach the power broker. Awareness creates positive results. Keep in mind that awareness of the environment is developed over time and is the result of continuously assessing the needs and demands of the school environment.

Reliable information is sometimes difficult to discern. That is why school librarians guide learners to determine if bias is woven into data. A great deal of evidence can be collected when problem solving, but large quantities of data do not necessarily *prove* anything. There is a need to sift through evidence before reaching a conclusion about a situation. Without a careful scan of evidence, proof may be based on assumptions grounded in faulty reasoning. Proof is the final statement, and evidence is the information that helps to establish truth. A district school librarian supervisor was told by the superintendent that he was going to tell the school board that learners would see the school librarian more if they were on a fixed schedule. The district supervisor collected data that proved the exact opposite. The data showed that multiple classes and a larger number of walk-in learners received services from the school librarian when a flexible schedule was implemented. One of the most powerful examples was a middle school librarian who provided a library orientation to the entire school. As a result, classes were blocked from the school librarian's expertise for more than two months while scheduled orientation classes filled the library time and spaces. The next year the school librarian provided orientation to learners through their science classes using meaningful research as an opportunity to integrate library information into the learners' first library visit. When statistics were gathered, the total number of classes and learners who received school library services via science classes more than doubled. The superintendent's evidence assumed that every child would be assured of a moment with the school librarian each week. The proof of more time in the school library came from evidence based on authentic data.

## Connecting to the Shared Foundations

For school librarians, making sound decisions to benefit instruction and the overall school library requires relating to the ideas central to problem solving. The ideas are reinforced in the Create Domain in the Frameworks for School Librarians and School Libraries, especially in the Shared Foundations of Inquire, Curate, and Explore. Designing and implementing activities and lessons based on the specific Competencies and Alignments listed in these Shared Foundations enhance the opportunity to teach problem-solving skills. These intentionally designed lessons and activities counter the learner's natural reaction to accept quick answers by purposely developing problem-solving skills through use of "cycles of design, implementation, and reflection" (AASL 2018a, 51).

### INQUIRE

The Key Commitment of the Inquire Shared Foundation states, "Build new knowledge by inquiring, thinking critically, identifying problems, and developing strategies for solving problems" (AASL 2018a, 68). When school librarians focus on the inquiry process, learning becomes more authentic. All stakeholders feel the impact when the culture of asking questions and finding answers is cultivated in the school library.

"School librarians promote new knowledge generation by facilitating the development of products that illustrate learning" (AASL 2018a, School Librarian I.B.3.). A product is not limited to a thing but is expanded to mean the result of problem solving. Solutions can be anything from concrete products to methods with actions.

A tangible problem-solving result may be the creation of a 3-D machine. A research plan demonstrates solving a problem by using a method with subsequent actions. The spectrum of products that learners may develop illustrates powerful learning through problem solving.

What products can school librarians develop in order to teach learners, including classroom educators, the benefits of problem solving? Perhaps the most important product that the school librarian can design is a well-developed instructional plan. The instructional plan needs to include an essential question, preferably generated by the learners; deliberate, well-thought-out activities that incorporate appropriate resources to address the learner's needs; and an environment that encourages the inquiry process. School librarians need to give learners opportunities, both structured and unstructured, to work through the inquiry process to solve problems. Learners who show growth in this skill set should be a goal of the school librarian and the result of a strong instructional plan. Classroom educators benefit from designing and implementing sound instructional plans when school librarians fulfill the roles of instructional partner and information specialist.

School libraries, under the leadership of the school librarian, serve as a valuable resource and supporter of extracurricular activities for the larger school community. Because of its accessibility to resources and environment encouraging involvement, "the school library enables generation of new knowledge by supporting flexible scheduling to provide learner and educator access to staff and resources at the point of need" (AASL 2018a, School Library I.B.2.). An example of stakeholders who exemplify this Alignment are learners and classroom educators (as sponsors) who participate in robotics competitions. They both appreciate and realize the scope of the school library to model the inquiry process and develop a product to illustrate learning. When given a challenge, robotics team members must work together to design a robot to solve a problem. At a deeper level, they must identify the problem, assess and organize data, and propose and organize an action plan. They must accomplish all these tasks while working on a strict schedule to develop an innovative machine that incorporates members' ideas. And, key to the competition, learners hope to win a prize. Important to each robotic team's success is to evaluate and reflect on the results in order to improve the product before the competition ends. This example shows the importance of using the school library to develop problem-solving skills that extend outside the physical space.

## CURATE

Bernard Marr (2018), a reporter for *Forbes* magazine, wrote an article titled "How Much Data Do We Create Every Day? The Mind-Blowing Stats Everyone Should Read." The following statistics from Marr's article are important to remember as school librarians design instructional plans and curriculum:

- Over the last two years alone, 90 percent of the data in the world was generated.
- On average, Google now processes more than 40,000 searches *every* second (3.5 billion searches per day)!
- While 77% of searches are conducted on Google, it would be remiss not to remember other search engines are also contributing to our daily data generation. Worldwide there are 5 billion searches a day.

Given such statistics, one of the most important skills that school librarians teach, through modeling and formal instruction, is the ability of learners to organize resources and gather information. "School librarians promote information gathering appropriate to the task by providing tools and strategies to organize information by priority, topic, or other systematic scheme" (AASL 2018a, School Librarian IV.B.4.). Self-assessment tools include rubrics or checklists to use during the inquiry process. Another strategy is to follow logical questioning sequences to help complete graphic organizers to synthesize gathered information. Given the amount of information available, it is imperative for learners to develop the skills to organize the gathered information to fully complete the problem-solving process.

As information specialists and teachers, school librarians identify the need for educators at the building and district levels to learn the skills needed to apply the available resources to the curriculum-based project or topic. By designing and providing professional development, school librarians equip educators with tools and strategies to incorporate organization and sound research processes in the classroom. To achieve this Alignment, "the school library promotes selection of appropriate resources and tools for information use by providing opportunities for all members of the school community to develop information and technology skills needed to promote the transfer of information-related problem-solving strategies across all disciplines" (AASL 2018a, School Library IV.B.2.). As a result of effective professional development, the administration and classroom educators continue to realize the purpose of the school library.

## EXPLORE

School librarians realize that the skills needed for problem solving are not developed or used in isolation but are improved when implemented in a cycle, as explained in the Create Competency for school librarians. "School librarians stimulate learners to construct new knowledge by teaching problem solving through cycles of design, implementation, and reflection" (AASL 2018a, School Librarian V.B.1.). This specific Competency extends the effectiveness of the Explore Key Commitment: "Discover and innovate in a growth mindset developed through experience and reflection" (AASL 2018a, 104).

One of the most familiar examples of learners' use of the cycle of design, implementation, and reflection in the school library is the research process. During formal instruction, best practice is for school librarians to provide learners an opportunity to brainstorm and organize their thoughts and the steps involved to complete the project during the initial design of the project. Providing graphic organizers such as T charts, organization-focused websites, or note-taking apps to organize ideas promotes the thought process. Being meticulous and paying attention to this design step saves time and stress and allows the overall research process to be successful.

In the second step of the cycle—implementation—learners take time to identify, access, and navigate available resources, both print and digital. Choosing reliable and valid information to satisfy the learner's need and understanding the ethical use of the resources are key parts of the implementation step. Learners are more empowered to genuinely become involved in this step when the school librarian takes time to model its importance.

The last step—reflection—is crucial to the learner's experience but sometimes does not happen because of lack of time. Giving learners time to assess the overall research process brings closure to a project and provides a sense of satisfaction. One component of assessment and reflection is self-assessment by the learners of their research question, resources and specific information chosen, and the product developed to illustrate learning.

Another example is the choosing of materials for pleasure reading. Learners, whether consciously or unconsciously, go through a cycle of design, implementation, and reflection to maximize their choices and experiences of reading. The cycle begins with designing a plan to make decisions about what they want to read to meet their current need. They choose fiction or nonfiction, print or digital based on availability, and format—graphic novel or prose—based on preference. These decisions in the cycle of design are important because they influence the success of the chosen material.

Once material is chosen, learners read all of it, internalizing whether the material is meeting their needs. The learner may want to skim the material to get a quick answer, if searching for information, or skim the novel quickly to identify story elements. This desire, driven by either instinct or time, does the learner and the material a disservice. It is optimal for learners to take the time to read the material in its entirety to ensure finding quality information or enjoying the story.

After reading, the learner reflects on the material based on the need being met, the enjoyment level, and possible considerations for further reading. This reflection step is critical to the development of problem-solving and decision-making skills because it provides closure to the cycle. It allows learners to determine whether their initial decisions in designing a plan were correct and whether they analyzed the material in depth to maximize its use. This step also affects the next materials chosen by the learner, either for pleasure or for assignment purposes.

As the information specialist at the building level, the school librarian identifies the value of the school library to have emerging technologies available to facilitate the cycle of design, implementation, and reflection. It is the responsibility of the school librarian to do research on which technologies best meet the needs of the school community and to allocate space and monetary resources to them. "The school librarian works with appropriate stakeholders to ensure that learners have access to devices and applications that best support all learners' abilities to demonstrate learning" (AASL 2018a, 108). These emerging technologies ensure the ability of all stakeholders to become more confident in their problem-solving skills.

## Effective Problem Solving

Problem solving is fundamental to sound decision making, even though decisions are frequently handled as an automatic reaction to a need. The best solutions result from school librarians' intentional use of a four-step problem-solving process that includes a method to identify the problem, gather data, implement a solution, then evaluate and reflect on the results. When school librarians are aware of the different styles of decision making that fall into the categories of emotional decisions, quick decisions, or data-driven decisions, they can improve their own problem-solving strategies. Key to effective problem solving is developing situational awareness and assessing the environment of the school and its power brokers. Anticipating the reaction of the educational community is essential to implementing a problem-solving solution. In addition, collecting information is vital to successful problem-solving, and school librarians must ensure that the data or evidence collected is vetted and reviewed. Incomplete analysis of the evidence can lead to flawed assumptions and poor decisions. Through practice of the problem-solving process, school librarians will live the ideas reinforced in the Create Domain in the AASL Standards Frameworks for School Librarians and School Libraries, especially in the Shared Foundations of Inquire, Curate, and Explore.

# 5

# Critical Thinking

C ritical thinking is directly related to decision making and is different from problem solving because it relies on reflection and deep reasoning. Problem solving is more analytical in reviewing data and information to determine trends and patterns. Critical thinking requires deeper consideration to reach a comprehensive conclusion about data and information that should challenge ideas and assumptions. Critical thinking facilitates understanding logical connections between ideas; identifying, constructing, and evaluating arguments; and detecting inconsistencies and common mistakes in reasoning (Lau and Chan, n.d.). Improving critical-thinking skills is central to school librarians' success as managers and educators. As managers school librarians make decisions that impact school library services for educators and learners. In addition, school librarians are expected "to design and teach engaging inquiry-based learning experiences as well as assessments that incorporate multiple literacies and foster critical thinking" (AASL 2018a, 174). Critical thinking is a core competency that school librarians must refine.

Understanding logical connections between ideas results when critical thinking is present. Knowing how to interpret conclusions by use of reason makes decisions stronger. Logic and critical thinking are fundamental to many disciplines, including science, mathematics, and computer science. *Logic* is defined by *Merriam-Webster* as "the science that deals with the formal principles of reasoning."[1] When a school librarian is presented with multiple statements of facts and information, it is important to sift through the data to find commonalities as well as conflicts. Determining a logical connection between ideas creates meaning between causes and the resulting outcomes. Figure 4.2 in the preceding chapter provided the Ishikawa or Fishbone Diagram method for determining cause and effect. Another way to determine cause and effect is to use the 5 whys technique (figure 5.1) whereby the school librarian continues to ask why until a meaningful conclusion is reached. Creating a

**FIGURE 5.1**

## The 5 whys technique

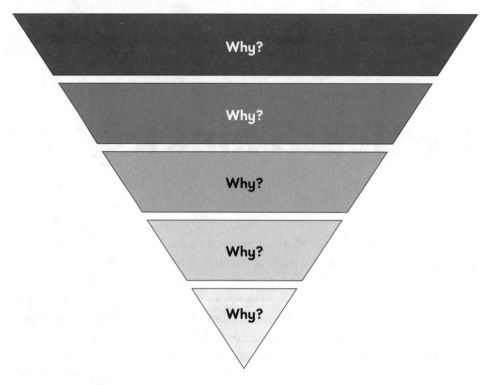

flowchart also visually indicates cause and effect. Brainstorming with colleagues is another method to determine cause and effect (Elmansy 2018). Once finished with identifying all the causes and resulting effects that impact a decision, it is important to organize the related concepts and ideas. It is essential for the school librarian to utilize critical-thinking skills to determine a logical relationship between the data collected (causes) and the resulting assumptions (effects) because from this analysis an action plan will evolve.

## Finding Commonalities

Important factors in decision making are identifying, constructing, and evaluating arguments. Improving one's quality of thought results each time a viewpoint is evaluated because arguments are based on a belief that may or may not be true. The developer of the argument may have his own objectives and purposes for convincing others to accept his perspective. If a school librarian constructs a rationale for a school-wide technology day, then the next step is to identify connections to the school improvement plan and the need for authentic use of technology. A physical plan for the day that includes a time line, areas of the school impacted, numbers and types of technology devices, and the software programs to be used should then be outlined. As part of the evaluation of the anticipated program, the objectives for the event are refined to ensure that there are expected benefits for learners. The purpose of explaining the objectives and benefits of the program is to convincingly assure the school community of the value of a technology day. Before the plan is presented to stakeholders, each segment of the day is reviewed and an evaluation of the rationale for the day is completed. Developing a school-wide event reinforces critical-thinking skills by weaving an instructional idea into the educational goals of the school. In addition, logical and logistical thinking are required to manage an event that includes the entire educational community. The school librarian uses critical-thinking skills to reach this point in championing and implementing a technology day.

## Finding Inconsistencies

Critical thinking is the ability to detect inconsistencies and common mistakes in reasoning. This skill is essential for school librarians when making decisions and directing a library. Managing a school library brings many requests and unique ideas to evaluate. For example, an administrator asked to use the school library as a testing site. The rationale was that the school library is a large, quiet area that can accommodate a large group of students. Using the school library may have seemed like a great idea to the administrator, but the resulting consequences for instruction needed to be assessed. In addition to evaluating the request, the savvy school librarian must be diplomatic as well as convincing with a response.

This school librarian thoughtfully assessed the request. There were several inconsistencies in the administrator's reasoning. The first point, that the school library served a large number of students, was correct; however, all the tables sat four students who would be in proximity to each other, presenting a testing security problem. So, the reasoning that a large room was automatically a great testing site was just not quite accurate. As for a quiet place, nothing could be farther from the truth because the school library served as a gathering spot for educators and learners between classes. In addition, educators and learners would constantly be going in and out with requests for materials and technology needs. Even though the school librarian identified inconsistencies and common mistakes in the reasoning to use the school library for testing, she recognized that none of these arguments would overturn the administrator's desire to close the school library. The school librarian knew that identifying and constructing a rebuttal explaining that the library was not an ideal testing site would not change the request. As a result, she consulted with other educators in the school to create a solution that would provide testing for large numbers of students without interrupting instruction in the library. Four classes were scheduled to be in the school library during the testing window. Each of the educators agreed to have learners meet at the school library for that day. This approach opened four classroom spaces with individual desks in a quiet environment. Because the administrator's request was reviewed logically for inconsistencies and mistakes in reasoning, the school librarian was able to construct a deeper, more thought-provoking solution. The administrator was pleased with the identification of four classrooms to be used for the testing, and, as a result, the school library remained available for the entire population of more than 1,500 learners.

## Developing Critical-Thinking Skills

"Critical thinking is, in short, self-directed, self-disciplined, self-monitored, and self-corrective thinking" (Paul and Elder 2008). For this reason, inquiry and questioning skills are key to developing critical thinking. The process of inquiry supported through higher level questioning encourages ingenuity, creativity, and innovation because it takes thoughts from a basic level to an unconventional, original idea. School librarians are charged with "establishing and supporting a learning environment that builds critical-thinking and inquiry dispositions for all learners" (AASL 2018a, School Library I.D.1.). If deep inquiry begins with developing questioning skills, then school librarians must be intentional when incorporating higher level questions into analysis of a decision to be made. Leveled questions are key to solid analysis of a situation because information is gathered from basic-level questioning and develops meaning by increasing the depth of questioning. Asking thoughtful questions encourages and stimulates a higher level of the cognitive processes. School librarians who practice inquiry and higher level questioning skills strengthen the disposition of critical thinking and become self-directed, self-disciplined, self-monitored, and self-corrective thinkers.

When school librarians establish and support "a learning environment that builds critical-thinking and inquiry dispositions for all learners," that goal is sometimes thwarted by learners' own acceptance of an immediate answer to a question or problem (AASL 2018a, School Library I.D.1.). These immediate answers are a concern for school librarians who encourage learners to challenge their own assumptions before making quick decisions. Learners live in a fast-paced environment in which answers, video games, and apps provide immediate satisfaction. Failure to use the processes of cross-checking information and triangulation prevents learners from challenging quick answers. There is a solution for school librarians. They can encourage information sharing, which results in deeper analysis. Incorporating collaboration activities into lessons provides an opportunity for learners to "think critically as they comment, elaborate in response to questions, and question other learners. Being confronted with diverse viewpoints and alternative interpretations of a situation or problem improves critical-thinking and problem-solving strategies" (AASL 2018a, 86).

School librarians have incorporated critical thinking into instruction ever since *Information Power* was released in 1988 and defined one role of the school librarian as teacher (AASL 2018a, 6). The need for learners to think critically is extremely important in today's educational environment in which assessment tools indicate a school's accreditation and impact learners' graduation. Standardized test questions incorporate critical thinking, and so success for educators, learners, and their schools is more dependent on preparing learners to think critically. Violet H. Harada and Joan M. Yoshina encouraged school librarians to assess for critical understanding. Among the skills they encouraged school librarians to monitor are

> assessing ability to connect new learning to prior knowledge, assessing ability to ask a range of questions to focus the search for understanding, assessing ability to consider different points of view toward a controversial issue before coming to a conclusion, assessing ability to identify bias, assessing ability to draw conclusions, and assessing ability to effectively communicate understanding. (Harada and Yoshina 2010, 101–115)

Each of these skill areas when targeted by school librarians increases learners' critical-thinking and decision-making ability over time.

## Connecting to the Shared Foundations

The beginning of each school year provides school librarians the opportunity to use their own critical-thinking and overall decision-making skills and apply those skills to their practice. Taking the time to self-assess strengths and weaknesses in the school library to help develop professional and personal goals requires intentional deeper analysis inherent in critical thinking. School librarians foster critical-thinking and overall decision-making skills in themselves because the skills benefit instruction and expand how the learners process newly acquired skills and information. The focus on developing critical-thinking skills is evident throughout the *National School Library Standards for Learners, School Librarians, and School Libraries* in the Common Beliefs, Shared Foundations, Key Commitments, Domains, Competencies, and Alignments.

## INQUIRE

Specifically, in the Create Domain of the Shared Foundation Inquire in the *AASL Standards Framework for School Librarians,* "School librarians promote new knowledge generation by devising and implementing a plan to fill knowledge gaps" (AASL 2018a, School Librarian I.B.2.). Identifying and addressing the knowledge gaps in the school library require critical-thinking skills. At the different levels, the lesson content may vary, but the intentional focus to devise and implement an authentic plan to fill knowledge gaps is the same. When school librarians are conscious of addressing knowledge gaps, learners realize that the quick answer may not always be correct. Generally, the correct, quality answer and development of skills take effort and time.

At the elementary level, school librarians realize that they must purposefully address one important knowledge gap—learners' and educators' use of the online school library catalog to search for resources. Learners and educators must develop not only the skill of creating an effective catalog search but also the ability to read the search results for important information, such as availability, location, and other enclosed data. Creating structured lessons and providing unstructured opportunities, through open access checkout, for learners to use the online school library catalog stimulate learners' interest in using the catalog. The structured lessons could include process, modeling, and practice by having learners collaborate to choose a topic to search, create a search, and take a picture on a tablet to show the success of the search.

At the secondary level, learners' understanding of the reasons for citing sources and the tools available to do so is a knowledge gap. School librarians also recognize the knowledge gap of choosing authentic information sources to meet the learner's need. That need could be to acquire information for a school-based assignment or to explore a personal interest. Either way, learners need to be taught to consciously ask reliability and truthfulness questions when choosing sources. School librarians, in collaboration with classroom educators in different disciplines, model choosing and citing sources through structured lessons and projects and empower learners and educators to do the same. Having learners develop their critical-thinking skills to recognize the need to choose and cite sources enhances the research process.

Although learners' acquisition of information to fill knowledge gaps is important, the school library, under the leadership of the school librarian, realizes the need for all stakeholders to feel the instructional impact of the school library. "The school library enables generation of new knowledge by providing experiences with and access to resources, information, ideas, and technology for all learners in the school community" (AASL 2018a, School Library I.B.1.). This goal is reinforced when school librarians provide in-service sessions for parents who are concerned about digital citizenship, professional development sessions after school for educators, and evening PTA events that concentrate on increasing literacy through resources. School librarians also address this Alignment when the school library's virtual presence is amplified through school-wide communications. School-wide communications can be spread by administrators, classroom educators, and learners, depending on the school population, so the larger school community is able to access the available resources. This amplification of resources and how to access them helps the school community to apply critical-thinking skills outside the physical space.

## CURATE

The choosing of information sources also connects to the Create Domain for the Shared Foundation Curate in the *AASL Standards Framework for School Librarians*. "School librarians promote information gathering appropriate to the task by fostering the questioning and assessing of validity and accuracy of information" (AASL 2018a, School Librarian IV.B.3.). The term *validity* is a derivative of the word *valid,* which means "well-grounded or justifiable: being at once relevant and meaningful."[2] Validity relates to how relevant and meaningful the information is for the learner's needs. *Accuracy* is a derivative of the word *accurate,* which means "free from error especially as the result of care."[3] Accuracy relates to how truthful the source and information are. In a study conducted by the Massachusetts Institute of Technology and published in March 2018, scientists found that "fake news and false rumors reach more people, penetrate deeper into the social network, and spread much faster than accurate stories" (Meyer 2018). "'It seems to be pretty clear [from our study] that false information outperforms true information,' said Soroush Vosoughi, a data scientist at MIT who has studied fake news since 2013 and who led this study" (Meyer 2018). Because many learners rely on social media to get information, school librarians need to create opportunities, both structured and unstructured, in the school library for learners to use deeper critical-thinking questions and analysis to choose information sources. "The school library promotes selection of appropriate resources and tools for information use by demonstrating and documenting how resources and technology are used to address information needs" (AASL 2018a, School Library IV.B.1.). Structured opportunities for such demonstration include formal collaborative lessons and small-group help in the school library. As instructional partner, the school librarian works with classroom educators to design and implement lessons that model how resources are used to find questions and fill information holes. As information specialist, the school librarian develops innovative ways to demonstrate and document how best to use what the school library offers. "The creation of user supports that act as tutorials for independent research skills and other information-seeking activities facilitate[s] users' seeking ways to incorporate resources collection into practice, including use of social media sites" (AASL 2018a, 99). Unstructured opportunities include open access study time during and after school. Learners will feel success during the research process the more often they pick effective sources because of their critical-thinking skills.

## EXPLORE

The Create Domain in the Shared Foundation Explore of the *AASL Standards Framework for School Librarians* describes a different way to develop critical-thinking skills when "school librarians stimulate learners to construct new knowledge by providing opportunities for tinkering and making" (AASL 2018a, School Librarian V.B.2.). EBSCO, a provider of databases and e-learning resources, published an article in August 2017 titled *Makerspaces: Hands-on Learning for Students of All Abilities.* "Through making, students of varying abilities learn and develop new skills like critical thinking and problem solving, communication and collaboration. Makerspaces provide a catalyst for all students to strengthen these skills, which can lead to success in other areas of school, work, and life" (EBSCO 2017). The resources provided in and the philosophy behind makerspaces encourage learners to make their ideas into reality, often using project-based learning to make an authentic connection to the curriculum. When school librarians design the physical space and lessons to incorporate more makerspace opportunities that implement technology as a tool or resource for learning, learners develop their deeper critical-thinking skills as they problem solve to create their ideas (AASL 2018a, School Library V.B.1.).

Makerspaces offer all stakeholders opportunities to develop critical-thinking skills through experience. School librarians realize the importance of establishing physical and virtual spaces to encourage critical thinking. "The school library facilitates construction of new knowledge by ensuring that multiple learning activities can occur in both physical and virtual spaces" (AASL 2018a, School Library V.B.2.). The organization of these spaces, for technology use as well as accessibility, to support and enhance each other allows stakeholders, educators, and parents to maximize their use of resources.

## Constructing Critical Thinking

Critical thinking is an integral part of decision making because it requires deeper, more intentional thinking and makes the results of the decisions richer. The school library provides both structured and unstructured opportunities for school librarians, educators, and learners to develop critical-thinking skills. The purpose of critical thinking is to make better decisions that result in positive outcomes for the school library. School librarians who understand how they think consider all options. They analyze the rationale behind stakeholder arguments to determine commonalities and inconsistencies in their logic before making final decisions. Whether the decisions are about designing instructional lessons, allocating funds for resources, or utilizing space for makerspaces, school librarians use and foster critical-thinking skills in themselves and stakeholders to maximize the school library. This repeated use of critical-thinking strategies by school librarians to administer the library, form instructional strategies, and make personal decisions reinforces the Competencies and Alignments in the Create Domain in the AASL Standards Frameworks for School Librarians and School Libraries, especially in the Shared Foundations of Inquire, Curate, and Explore. The Competencies and Alignments in turn reinforce higher level thinking and encourage growth of the dispositions needed to make sound decisions. School librarians will continue to model and promote the challenges and benefits of developing critical-thinking skills as the amount of information available increases and the need to make quality, not quick, decisions remains important.

**NOTES**

1. https://www.merriam-webster.com/dictionary/logic
2. https://www.merriam-webster.com/dictionary/valid
3. https://www.merriam-webster.com/dictionary/accurate

# Emotional Resilience

# 6

**H**enry Ford once said, "Failure is only the opportunity to begin again more intelligently" (Salzberg 2015, 110). This statement becomes real when learners are empowered to become engaged with the research process in the school library. They realize that the quick answer is not necessarily the best or most complete answer and that it takes time to dig deeper to find richer, more thorough information and satisfying results. Emotional resilience ties into decision making because the way learners react to roadblocks in the research process affects further decisions they make, whether about which topic to pursue or which resources to choose. Emotional resilience significantly impacts learners' decisions and how they handle academic obstacles.

An elementary school librarian incorporated assessment into each of her instructional lessons. A first-grade class was finishing research for a project. Learners used presentation software whereby slides were populated with the information the learners located. As part of the assessment, the school librarian asked learners to describe what they did when they could not find the information they needed. She was assessing for emotional resiliency. Learners' answers ranged from "I didn't cry or stomp my foot" to "I asked the librarian for help." Learners' answers indicated awareness that roadblocks in research have solutions and that trial and error are part of the research process. This school librarian provided a safe environment for her learners to effectively build emotional resilience. In addition, it was clear that the learners understood that their school librarian was a support system available for them if they encountered difficulty when researching. The disposition of emotional resilience fosters persistence and is key to productive research and academic success for learners. Development of emotional resilience is also an essential disposition for school librarians as they perform the interrelated roles of leader, instructional partner, information specialist, teacher, and program administrator.

*Resilience* is defined by the *Oxford Dictionary* as "the capacity to recover quickly from difficulties; toughness."[1] The *Richmond Times-Dispatch* published an article by Dr. Robert Cross (2013) in which he explained that "resilience—the ability to bounce back from difficulties—is a trait that can be improved by developing strategies for dealing with hardships." School librarians engage learners in strategies such as identifying multiple sources of information, working with others to create solutions to problems, and sharing with others any obstacles encountered during the research process. One of Dictionary.com's definitions of *resiliency* is interesting when applied to the school library: "the power or ability to return to the original form, position, etc., after being bent, compressed, or stretched; elasticity."[2] Once learners realize the power and success of practicing emotional resilience, their mindset will not be able to return to the original point of uncertainty where they simply went through the motions of the research process. They will no longer be focused on the problems related to research but will be challenged to expand their information seeking, leading to deeper learning. Emotional resilience is a life skill that provides learners the endurance to cope with personal as well as academic setbacks.

## Perceiving Possibilities

Just as learners must be ready to change a research plan, the school librarian must be ready to adapt to an administrative directive. This capacity for change requires an understanding of the power behind developing emotional resilience so that good decisions and effective solutions move the school library in a positive direction. For school librarians, identifying what can be controlled in the environment is connected to emotional resilience and decision making. This identifying process affects what school librarians choose as stress triggers as related to the school library. It also provides the school librarian opportunities to create alternative solutions to tough requests. For example, when nonnegotiable situations occur, school librarians realize that they need to put their time and energy in another project. At the building level, a nonnegotiable may be the delegation of duties that are not instructional. School librarians sometimes need to step back from a directive such as bus duty so they can mindfully reflect on what can be learned from the mandate. For example, when a school librarian returned from summer break, she was placed on hall duty at the start of every day. This requirement created major inconvenience for learners and educators who expected assistance with printing and finding resources. The school librarian went to the school administrator to request that the duty be modified or changed. He would not budge. So the school librarian stuck it out for an entire year. She then returned to the administrator to volunteer for an alternative duty for the next school year that would not impact the learners' and educators' library needs. He was agreeable. By timing a follow-up request to the administrator that was a schedule he could work with, the school librarian succeeded in being removed from the duty roster the next year. After the first meeting with her administrator, she realized that she needed to put her time and energy into the school library. This awareness relieved stress and led her to a creative solution for the future. In another example, district decisions, such as changing the selection policy to incorporate a school district belief, may be in direct conflict with principles of intellectual freedom. A district supervisor faced with this situation engaged emotional resiliency by sidestepping the actual request and writing the belief into the purchasing guidelines in a handbook rather than making it part of the school board's selection policy. Thus, the district supervisor transformed a nonnegotiable into an acceptable solution. In each of these examples, the school librarian and the district supervisor practiced emotional resilience by either adapting or being resourceful. By being mentally tough and taking ownership of adversity, school librarians display the emotional resilience that impacts their decisions and psyches.

## Handling Political Ambiguity

Decision making requires flexibility. When a school librarian works in an educational community, it is extremely important to understand the changing nature of a political environment. To be flexible when making decisions, the school librarian must develop emotional resiliency by understanding the underlying causes of instability in the school. Uncertainty may be the result of procedures, policies, or rules that are unclear or that do not seem to fit a situation (Bolman and Deal, n.d.). School librarians develop emotional resilience when they follow operational guidelines created by administrators even when the rules may not seem efficient or effective. For example, if a principal expects new programs or ideas to be presented to a leadership team, then the school librarian needs to present important data to the leadership team even when that team delays implementation. If the principal prefers that educators go to an assistant principal first, then the school librarian is required to follow that established protocol to be successful in the school. School librarians must recognize that problems arise in a political environment when power is concentrated in the wrong place or when power is so dispersed that results are unpredictable (Bolman and Deal, n.d.). So how can this inconsistency be countered by a school librarian? First, alliances and advocates must be identified and nurtured. Then the school librarian must use negotiating skills to bring educators together to achieve a desired objective. Working collaboratively with others provides opportunities for give and take. At the same time, the school librarian develops flexibility by seeking others' ideas and solutions. The decisions that result often expand school library initiatives to a larger group of learners and departments in the school. Instability in the work environment challenges the comfort level of the school librarian. As stress increases, school librarians who become creative problem solvers increase their emotional resilience capacity and conquer stress through resourcefulness.

## *Practicing Patience*

Confidence and awareness are impacted when school librarians allow negative comments, disagreeable situations, and transformational change to mess with their psyche. Part of living is knowing that events will occur that create uncomfortable feelings and generate fear. Comments that challenge school librarians' decisions should be expected when people hear a reply they do not like. It takes awareness to understand that a negative comment is attacking the credibility of a decision. Staying calm and refraining from arguing develop emotional resilience by removing the school librarian's tendency to justify the option suggested. Practicing self-control results in an awareness of the underlying concerns of all parties involved in the decision. The process of pausing, listening, reassessing, and then reacting builds emotional resilience and confidence. It is an opportunity to step back and compose thoughts about the situation so that a less emotional reaction occurs. When working through disagreeable situations, it may be necessary to validate the feelings and ideas of those who are concerned. Showing empathy does not mean the school librarian should change a decision; rather, it creates an opportunity for discussion and lowers the intensity of emotions, thus generating more positive feelings. Another option when faced with negative comments or disagreeable situations is to ignore them. This approach may be best if the school librarian is upset and concerned, because walking away provides cooldown time. A school librarian was upset when another educator chose to keep her class out of the library after the learners misbehaved in the classroom. The educator felt that this punishment was best because her class loved the school library, and her goal was to decrease unwanted behavior by taking away something the learners enjoyed. Instead of confronting the educator in the presence of the learners, forcing the educator to defend her actions in front of them, the school librarian showed emotional resilience and waited. At the end of the day, she went to the educator's room to discuss openly, one-on-one, the negative impact of using the school library as a punishment. The school librarian explained that she was uncomfortable with the school library being used as punishment for learners' misbehavior in another area of the school. The educator agreed. In this situation, the school librarian's self-control and patience had a far superior result, and the educator never again attempted to use the school library as a punishment.

Another area that can impact a school librarian's confidence is transformational change. Resistance to change surfaces when educators must shift directions, particularly when they believe current instructional strategies are successful. This resistance to school library change can negatively impact school librarians' confidence. When school librarians are aware that resistance may occur, they will embrace their role of change agent. AASL provides the framework for transformational change through the *National School Library Standards.* In a sense the standards are key tools in the school librarian's toolbox. School librarians' confidence and emotional resilience are assisted when they use the AASL Standards and its supporting materials to guide instructional agendas. Confidence and awareness are strengthened when each negative comment, disagreeable situation, and move toward transformational change is confronted with patience. The calm projected by the school librarian is a direct result of emotional resilience.

### *Being Intentional and Less Reactive*

School librarians need to consciously identify their level of emotional resilience and then work to increase their ability to deal with adversity. Numerous news articles explain how an athlete, a politician, or a leader reacts emotionally to a situation, only to magnify any negative outcomes. These three situations are very different, but the common thread is a breakdown of emotional resilience. When a line judge calls a tennis ball out, a negative ad campaign maligns a politician, or a superintendent of a school district pulls a library book off the school library shelves, the results are twofold. First, a negative reaction based on emotional assumptions often intensifies the outcome of the decision. Second, the person responding emotionally often reacts without thinking through the situation, which results in a decision the person regrets.

Practicing strategies that develop emotional resilience is essential for sound decision making and effective administration of the school library. School librarians face a series of decisions as their day progresses. Body language and facial cues from the recipients of a decision may challenge the school librarian and elicit a confrontational answer. Echoed in the *National School Library Standards* is the fundamental leadership principle that it is more productive to accept different viewpoints and appreciate divergent thinkers. Alternatives encourage discussion and support deeper acceptance of decisions that are based on collaborative information. Each time a school librarian stops and thinks through a situation before responding, that librarian's emotional resilience is strengthened and the individual's decision making becomes intentional rather than reactive.

## Connecting to the Shared Foundations

How do school librarians promote emotional resilience in themselves and learners? Focusing on the Create Domain within the Inquire, Curate, and Explore Shared Foundations of the AASL Standards Frameworks for School Librarians and School Libraries, school librarians employ the Competencies and Alignments as a guide to develop lessons and activities that encourage the development of emotional resilience through authentic experiences. School librarians also realize the importance of developing and exercising emotional resilience to help improve their practice. Seizing opportunities through the five roles of a school librarian—leader, instructional partner, information specialist, teacher, and program administrator—is an excellent strategy to use to develop emotional resilience to benefit all stakeholders.

## INQUIRE

In the Create Domain of the Inquire Shared Foundation is the statement that "school librarians promote new knowledge generation by ensuring that learners probe possible answers to questions" (AASL 2018a, School Librarian I.B.1.). As teachers, school librarians provide learners a safe environment in which to fail and, more important, a support system of tools and skills to deal with the failure. Giving learners dedicated time to brainstorm possible answers before starting the research process empowers them to establish their own ideas. This research process could be for producing an informational report or choosing books for pleasure reading. Brainstorming can be done in handwritten, typed, or drawn responses. After the research process is complete, allowing learners to reflect on and compare their brainstormed possible answers to the newly acquired information affirms their ideas and brings closure to the process. This reflection contributes to the development of emotional resilience—even if finding the best information required many attempts, the learners continued to search and verified their original ideas. As program administrator, the school librarian creates a schedule that is conducive to instruction and that provides opportunities to develop emotional resilience. This function is supported in the Alignment, "The school library enables generation of new knowledge by supporting flexible scheduling to provide learner and educator access to staff and resources at the point of need" (AASL 2018a, School Library I.B.2.). When the schedule is flexible, allowing classes the necessary time to meet an instructional need, learners and educators are able to show growth in their mindset. The flexibility encourages time to effectively assess the skills being taught or to carefully choose materials for pleasure reading, depending on the need.

## CURATE

The Shared Foundation Curate is a powerful tool for building emotional resilience as one learns to "make meaning for oneself and others by collecting, organizing, and sharing resources of personal relevance" (AASL 2018a, 94). Emphasizing the personal relevance of the available resources for learners allows a real-life connection to be made and strengthened. In addition, two of the Competencies in the Create Domain of the *AASL Standards Framework for School Librarians* benefit learners as school librarians design lessons, "sharing a variety of sources" (AASL 2018a, School Librarian

IV.B.1.) and "encouraging the use of information representing diverse perspectives" (AASL 2018a, School Librarian IV.B.2.). Gathering and sharing ideas that represent different viewpoints promote emotional resilience as learners become open to ideas that are different from their own.

The first Competency of "sharing a variety of sources" allows school librarians and learners to ask pertinent questions, such as: What sources worked? What sources didn't work? Where should I look next to find a different source? This Competency also takes into account the fact that different formats appeal to different learning styles—digital versus print, book versus periodical, graphic novel versus prose. By being exposed to different formats, learners will realize for themselves which formats of sources best fit their needs.

The second Competency of "encouraging the use of information representing diverse perspectives" will result in richer information being selected and used by the learner. An example is how the authorship of a primary source affects the bias of the source. The learner needs to ask: Does the primary source support or deny my research question? Do I have sources that present each perspective? Does my research information present a complete picture of the topic? Finding quality information with diverse perspectives takes time, and when school librarians make a conscious effort to facilitate deeper searches and use of information, learners develop and enhance emotional resilience.

As information specialist and instructional partner, the school librarian has a responsibility to apply this concept of incorporating diverse perspectives when working with building- and district-level educators to maximize decisions that affect the school library. When collaborating with an educator, the school librarian proposes that the resources chosen be balanced with different perspectives to enrich the final products and models how to access the balanced resources. When promoting school library activities to administrators, showing how the chosen resources increase both emotional resilience and curriculum content skills bolsters the impact of the school library. This can be done through creating an infographic, interviewing learners and educators, and taking pictures and videos of learners' work.

The program administrator role emphasizes creating an environment that meets the needs of the larger school community. "The school library promotes selection of appropriate resources and tools for information use by designing and providing adequate, appropriate space for library resources, services, and activities" (AASL 2018a, School Library IV.B.5.). It is the conscious effort of the school librarian to structure a space that can facilitate different activities at once. When various stakeholders, including educators, learners, and parents, are able to access and use the school library at the same time, people realize the larger scope of the school library.

## EXPLORE

Having makerspaces in school libraries provides the materials and opportunities for school librarians and learners to achieve success in the Create Domain of the Shared Foundation Explore in the *AASL Standards Framework for School Librarians.* "School librarians stimulate learners to construct new knowledge by modeling persistence through self-directed tinkering and making" (AASL 2018a, School Librarian V.B.3.). When learners see school librarians being persistent with a maker project, struggling with the decisions that go into converting an idea into a 3-D reality, and striving to solve some of the problems that may arise with time or materials, learners appreciate the effort and time put into the project. When learners discuss with the school librarian the decisions made and process involved, the experience becomes richer for both parties. Learners realize that there can't always be a quick answer or that the quick answer is not always correct.

The design and implementation of makerspaces depend on the efficient allocation of physical space in the school library to facilitate both individual and group projects. "The school library facilitates construction of new knowledge by establishing and maintaining a learning environment conducive to independent and collaborative exploration and problem solving" (AASL 2018a, School Library V.B.3.). As a result, emotional resilience is developed unconsciously when stakeholders explore and learn in the school library.

## Advancing Emotional Resilience

Strengthening emotional resilience is essential for school librarians as they manage the school library. Decision making should not be hurried or reactionary but, instead, should be the result of a thoughtful and intentional response to a situation. Emotional resilience is taught to learners and educators as part of the school librarian's responsibilities. When the school librarian is performing the five roles of leader, instructional partner, information specialist, teacher, and program administrator, emotional resilience is a powerful disposition that impacts decisions, the school librarian's psyche, and the handling of adversity (figure 6.1). Emotional resilience is perceiving possibilities when options do not seem possible. Situations that evolve from the political environment in the school can cause uncertainty, so when school librarians maintain a calm and stable attitude, they create stability for flexible decision making. Emotional resilience involves directing the mind toward positive responses. Confidence increases when school librarians pause during decision making. Just as infusing wait time when asking learners a question increases the variety of responses, wait time with colleagues produces alternative thinking. Controlling the school environment is not always possible, but controlling responses to confrontations is a leadership skill that school librarians with strong emotional resilience can master.

FIGURE 6.1

## Outcomes of strengthening the disposition for emotional resilience

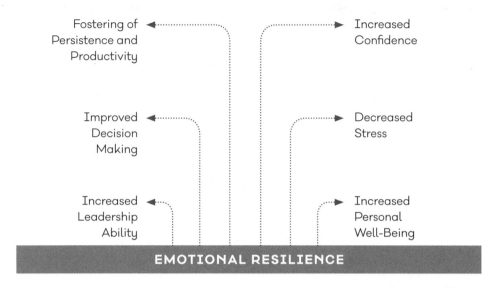

Adversity builds resilience. When school librarians face challenges, their courage, confidence, and strength emerge from deep inside, and they approach situations intentionally rather than reactively. The school library stakeholders benefit when learners, educators, and school librarians display persistence. Emotional resilience becomes primary to academic life. Understanding the importance of practicing the Competencies and Alignments from the Create Domain in the Inquire, Curate, and Explore Shared Foundations in the AASL Standards Frameworks for School Librarians and School Libraries and their relevance to developing emotional resilience will result in a high level of professional mastery. It is a solution to breaking learners' and educators' desire for a quick answer. And practicing these skills takes time. Just as athletes strengthen muscles for optimum performance, school librarians need to use the *National School Library Standards* to strengthen emotional resilience for maximum results for the library.

### NOTES

1. https://en.oxforddictionaries.com/definition/resilience
2. https://www.dictionary.com/browse/resilience?s=t

## Reflection Questions

Provide thoughtful answers to the following reflection questions using the lines provided.

How are your critical-thinking skills developed by using self-assessment tools?

_____

_____

Why is it important for you to follow a strategic process when problem solving?

_____

_____

How does intentional modeling by you as a school librarian affect the emotional resilience of your learners? Collaborators? Other stakeholders?

_____

_____

How are problem solving, critical thinking, and emotional resilience interrelated to support decision making?

_____

_____

What other Shared Foundations, Domains, and Competencies and Alignments in the AASL Standards Frameworks for School Librarians and School Libraries could you apply to decision making through problem solving, critical thinking, and emotional resilience? Explain how.

_____

_____

_____

## Self-Assessment

**Goal:** To self-assess my problem-solving, critical-thinking, and emotional resilience skills and then set goals to develop these skills for better decision making for the school library

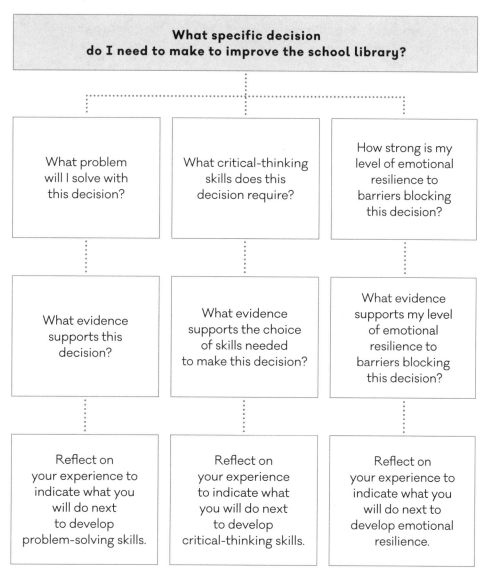

## Breakthrough Skills

There are three professional growth breakthrough skills to focus on that connect to problem solving, critical thinking, emotional resilience, and, ultimately, decision making. Being intentional when making decisions, taking time to find quality answers, and providing opportunities to model and practice make the stakeholders' school library experiences richer, empowering them to apply the decision-making skills outside school.

- **Be intentional** in the decisions made that impact the school library. How will this decision impact instruction? Who are the stakeholders impacted by this decision? What possible obstacles need to be addressed to implement this decision? When school librarians are intentional and focus on goals, problem solving becomes easier, critical-thinking skills are practiced to allow for deeper answers, and emotional resilience is improved.

- **Take time** to find quality answers. When school librarians model the behavior of not rushing to find basic answers, learners realize that quick doesn't always mean quality answers. Designing lessons that make time for asking questions, information-gathering and reflection expands the scope and depth of the results. Through authentic research time, learners will value the time needed for the research process.

- **Provide structured and unstructured opportunities** in the school library to be involved in the decision-making process. What real-life problems could the learners solve using the school library resources? Which critical-thinking skills could be developed with particular activities? How will the level of emotional resilience be strengthened in the school library? These structured and unstructured opportunities could include participating in formal and informal research, choosing books for pleasure reading, and using makerspaces.

# Communication

In the area of professional communication, school librarians do not just receive information but respond to, value, and organize ideas and initiatives that need to be shared. It is the school librarian's responsibility, as overall program administrator and leader, to decide if the ideas and initiatives need to be shared horizontally or vertically. In addition, the school librarian must determine the most effective plan for communicating with those affected by the ideas and initiatives. Communication tools change constantly, sometimes for the better and sometimes not. What does not change is the need for effective communication. Sharing knowledge and information within the educational community must be appropriate for those who are receiving the message. Deciding on a delivery method to disseminate information is dependent on the message content, the technology available, and the outcome needed. More important, school librarians understand that a message is impacted by the integrity of the sender and the clarity of the disclosed information. Effective communication requires integrity and clarity so that the sender succinctly conveys a message that the receiver interprets correctly. Integrity and clarity impact how messages are constructed and received whereas the method of sending the communication is key to how recipients interact with the information.

## A Communication Challenge for School Librarians

Achieving buy-in from educators, learners, and community members for the school library is a challenge at the school, district, state, and national levels. Without full acceptance by stakeholders, the value of the school library is diminished. There are ways to motivate stakeholders so the results are positive. When communicating, the

Competencies in the Domain Share from the Shared Foundations of Include, Curate, and Engage in the AASL Standards Frameworks for School Librarians and School Libraries provide opportunities for librarians to develop communication skills and impact stakeholders. School librarians are charged with "guiding learners [including educators] to contribute to discussions in which multiple viewpoints on a topic are expressed" (AASL 2018a, School Librarian II.C.2.). When this diversity happens, the discussions become richer and voices more authentic. School librarians realize the importance of collaborating in today's society, so they direct "learners [and educators] to join others to compare and contrast information" (AASL 2018a, School Librarian IV.C.3.).

As teachers, leaders, and information specialists, "school librarians promote the responsible, ethical, and legal sharing of new information with a global community by guiding the dissemination of new knowledge through means appropriate for the intended audience" (AASL 2018a, School Librarian VI.C.2.). This dissemination of new knowledge can come through structured and unstructured opportunities in the school library. Achieving this Competency allows stakeholders to contribute to the global community, utilizing the school library resources for legitimacy. In addition to crafting a clear message and analyzing the best method for delivering information, school librarians strengthen the disposition of integrity. These three components of communication are instrumental in supporting empowerment and engagement when seeking stakeholder buy-in.

# 7

# Integrity

**F**orbes **magazine reports the results of an annual Gallup poll that** determines which profession is the most trusted. For sixteen years, nurses were tops in the poll. Results in 2018 showed that "82 percent of Americans consider nurses to have high or very high honesty and ethical standards. Military officers come second with 71 percent saying they have high honesty standards while grade school teachers come third with 66 percent placing a high level of trust in them" (McCarthy 2018). At the other end of the poll, lobbyists were the least trusted. And with all the concern about fake news, newspaper and TV reporters scored low on the honesty poll, just above lawyers and business executives. Communicating authentic and honest information is valued whether it is from a nurse, someone from the business sector, or a school librarian. All professions benefit from honesty and trust. Integrity builds honesty and trust and is important to how educators view information they receive in communications from administrators, parents, and school librarians.

More important, integrity is critical to the success of school librarians as they serve in the role of program administrator and manage the school library. "The implementation of a successful school library program requires the collaborative development of the program mission, strategic plan, and policies" (AASL 2018a, 15). It is the responsibility and a requirement of the school librarian as program administrator and leader to ensure that school library initiatives, resources, and policies are communicated with integrity.

## Five Key Questions

The school librarian is often a one-person department, which makes it challenging to complete projects that require the support of other educators in the school. School library proposals and projects must be communicated in a language that educators understand while validating relevance to the larger educational community. How school librarians develop and strengthen integrity, what integrity looks like, why integrity is important to communication, where integrity benefits communication, and when integrity is appropriate are all issues that guide and strengthen the disposition of integrity.

## How Is Integrity Developed and Strengthened?

Several specific practices are involved in answering the question, How is integrity developed and strengthened? When communicating information, the school librarian must be aware of her personal values and beliefs. Examining whether these values and beliefs are aligned with AASL Common Beliefs is the first step to creating communications rooted in integrity. Before communicating with educators about a library program, the school librarian should review the AASL Common Beliefs and determine if there is one that is central to the proposed initiative. When the school librarian establishes a rationale that is consistent with the AASL Common Beliefs, she creates a reliable baseline for communicating to the educational community. For example, when two secondary school librarians wanted to extend collaboration to the Home and Family Sciences Department, they explained that as school librarians they believed that "learners should be prepared for college, career, and life" and that "fostering learners' personal interests and curricular mastery prepares them for success" (AASL 2018a, 12). This language from the AASL Common Beliefs provided talking points for the school librarians that targeted the values of the educators in the Home and Family Sciences Department. In the role of instructional partner, these school librarians followed up with suggestions for collaborative library experiences based on the Home and Family Sciences curriculum. Providing underlying principles such as those written in the AASL Common Beliefs ensures that the rationale is founded on ethical practices. Consequently, the integrity of the school librarian and the school library is consistently reinforced. Each collaborative experience deepens the disposition of integrity while building a reliable communication channel for the educational community.

## What Does Integrity Look Like?

As an instructional leader in the school, the school librarian must be able to answer the question, What does integrity look like? Integrity results from intentionally building a culture of academic honesty in the school library. This value is modeled by the school librarian through communications and instructional collaborations that influence the entire school community in a positive way. School librarians collaborate with educators on instructional and leadership issues in which tolerance of ideas is nurtured through "informed conversation and active debate" (AASL 2018a, School Librarian II.C.1.). Integrity is evident when the school librarian encourages diversity that is based on respectful, empathetic, and truthful information. When the school librarian nurtures ethics during the planning stage of instructional experiences, a culture of integrity develops. School librarians practice this culture with learners when they focus on the Competencies delineated in the Shared Foundation of Include. For example, when the school librarian allows differing viewpoints to be voiced in a safe environment such as the school library, empathy, respect, and tolerance become the norm (AASL 2018a, School Librarian II.B.1., II.B.2.). Educators and learners expect and anticipate a school librarian and school library environment grounded in fairness and objectivity because sensitivity, understanding, and awareness are exhibited in conversations. Empathy for learners' and educators' ideas provides opportunities for truth and accuracy to surface and strengthens the integrity of the school librarian. A strong culture of integrity modeled by the school librarian when serving in the roles of program administrator and instructional partner is extremely important to acceptance of information communicated to the educational community.

## *Why Is Integrity Important?*

The answer to the question, Why is integrity important in communications? is that integrity creates transparency and clears up ambiguity. For example, when questions arise after a school library announcement is made, the school librarian who provides honest answers creates stability in a confusing situation. School librarians who are leaders avoid surprises by seeking input from colleagues prior to announcing a change. Librarians obtain this input by providing collaborative teams of educators an opportunity to openly discuss initiatives in which change is anticipated. Leaders also create legitimacy for new programs by connecting the change to a core goal of the school, such as the school improvement plan. In each of these examples, integrity creates acceptance when an explanation for change is given that is trusted and respected. A district library supervisor needed to communicate to the elementary school librarians that learners would no longer be charged for lost materials. Each of the schools impacted by the decision included learners from low-income families. In addition, the federal programs supervisor agreed to supplement the school libraries with funding to replace lost materials. Knowing that discontinuing charges for lost books would be questioned, the district library supervisor called a meeting to communicate the new policy and procedure to the elementary school librarians face-to-face. The district supervisor began with research data on the importance of learners having access to good reading in their homes. Next, some anticipated concerns were introduced followed by discussion of ways to address these concerns. The elementary school librarians then participated in a brainstorming activity in which they identified positive methods to encourage responsible book return. The integrity of the district library supervisor created acceptance of this change because the elementary school librarians trusted that the rationale and need for the change were authentic and positive for learners. In addition, they believed that lost books would be replaced. The district supervisor brought a workable plan for replacing lost books that minimized the time school librarians would need to devote to implementing the new policy. The district library supervisor was open about the change, provided time for the school librarians to discuss concerns, and enabled them to be a part of the solution. Integrity of the communication brought positive results.

### *Where Is Integrity Important?*

The question, Where is integrity in communication important? has a simple answer: anywhere within the organizational structure of the school and district. As program administrator, the school librarian requires integrity to manage the school library effectively. For example, integrity is essential for acceptance and successful implementation of guidelines, policies, and procedures. These are foundational building blocks in the development of a school library that is organized and managed for access by users. Integrity is communicated by the school librarian daily through modeling ethical practices. When a school librarian is respectful and honest in communications, including instruction, a reputation for authenticity becomes rooted in reliable, straightforward, and sincere actions. Evidence of integrity is visible to stakeholders each time the school librarian follows through with requests and helps when asked. As a teacher the school librarian models integrity by properly citing sources in presentations, handouts, and information sharing where learners and educators are present. Educators appreciate the level of detail citations require, and, as a result, the intangible disposition of integrity is transformed into a concrete, visible model for the school community. Not only is integrity in communications important in daily activities and job responsibilities; it is also critical in face-to-face meetings in which discussion and pushback may occur. Communications to school board members, at teacher meetings, and with school administrators are instances in which consistently honest actions and remarks build trust for agreement and assistance with school library needs.

### *When Is Integrity Needed?*

Integrity is standard operating procedure for leaders. So the question, When is integrity in communication needed? has a simple answer—*always*. School librarians know that truthfulness is the most important character trait when communicating to educators and learners. Even when truth is perceived as bad news, frankness and sincerity provide listeners the reality of a situation or decision and enable them to better accept the information. In the school environment, the credibility of the school librarian rests on knowledge and information that is dependable even if it is not what educators want to hear. When truth is going to be received as bad news, timing is everything. Sharing the information before rumors begin to circulate provides an opportunity for school librarians to ensure that reactions are morphed into productive discussion. School librarians must be prepared to understand the impact that change has on educators and learners because recipients who expect change often react strongly. Leaders know how to frame change as a positive. This approach takes practice, and one way to create positive acceptance of change is to seek input, before a change is announced, from the members of the educational community that will be impacted. Educators' input may challenge a new library procedure or policy, but it also provides an opportunity for the school librarian to understand the perceived impact on specific groups in the school and modify the change.

## Barriers That Hinder Integrity

Obstacles occur that injure or impede integrity. If trust is lost, it is hard to get it back. Maintaining composure and professional commitment during difficult situations is needed when barriers to ethical situations arise. Sometimes in a political environment, integrity is attacked by decision makers. School librarians need to understand that educational leaders act based on their personal set of beliefs and values. If decision makers have incomplete information, then flaws in their decisions will ensue. An example of this breakdown occurred during the recent economic recession when a district library supervisor was asked to agree to downsizing the school librarians' contracts. The resulting reduction of contract days meant that school librarians, who were considered department chairs, would have a significant reduction in pay. The district library supervisor declined to agree to this request by central office administrators until the contracts and pay for all department heads across the district were evaluated. Taking a stand by asking for more information redirected the problem toward a better solution that would not have such a negative monetary impact on one segment of school personnel—in this case, the school librarians. During conversations with district leaders, the library supervisor maintained confidentiality about the situation and was sensitive to the pressures district leaders were operating under. The library supervisor's integrity was based on strong values of equity. So even though decision makers wanted a quick and easy solution to monetary shortfalls, the district library supervisor remained true to her beliefs, and, in the end, the final decision was fair to school librarians. More important, the district library supervisor's integrity remained intact. This was a strong play to preserve the integrity of the library supervisor and the school library positions.

## Connecting to the Shared Foundations

Using the AASL Standards Frameworks for School Librarians and School Libraries as guides, school librarians can better develop and practice their integrity to answer the questions related to communication. They realize the importance of using integrity, through actions and words, to strengthen the school library in the overall school environment. The Share Domain is the optimal domain to focus on because it emphasizes school librarians facilitating and promoting best practice in regard to diverse collections, collaboratively constructed sites, and information resources. The Shared Foundations of Include, Curate, and Engage identify vital Competencies and Alignments school librarians should meet for themselves as well as the school library, fostering stakeholder buy-in by addressing communication needs.

## INCLUDE

As school populations become more diverse and different cultures interact in schools, it is vital for school librarians to seize the opportunity for the school library to serve as a bridge for building communication among these many cultures. When school librarians model strong and inclusive communication skills and decisions for learners and fellow educators, the administration feels the positive impact. This impact is seen through instructional plans, well-rounded collections of print and digital resources, and an expectation of respect in the school library. As teachers and instructional partners, "school librarians facilitate experiences in which learners exhibit empathy and tolerance for diverse ideas by giving learners opportunities to engage in informed conversation and active debate" (AASL 2018a, School Librarian II.C.1.). Opportunities can be intentionally integrated into a lesson or occur spontaneously when people share ideas about content being studied, resources being evaluated, or books being chosen for pleasure reading. The integrity and communication skills developed through these conversations and debates illustrate that the school library fosters expression, tolerance, and the use of information to support ideas.

The importance of the school librarian in promoting and using well-rounded, strong collections to advocate for inclusion cannot be neglected. "The school library facilitates opportunities to experience diverse ideas by promoting the use of high-quality and high-interest literature in formats that reflect the diverse developmental, cultural, social, and linguistic needs of all learners and their communities" (AASL 2018a, School Library II.C.2.). The modeling of how to access these resources anytime and anywhere creates a connection to the larger community and meets the differentiated needs of the learners and educators.

"Constructing a learning environment that fosters the sharing of a wide range of viewpoints and ideas" encourages all stakeholders to thrive both personally and academically (AASL 2018a, School Library II.C.3.). When the school librarian uses integrity to communicate with a classroom educator about collaboration or with an administrator about data supporting a decision, the Include Shared Foundation is assimilated in the school library environment. The school librarian realizes the importance of modeling integrity in establishing the inclusive environment to maximize the role of the school library.

## CURATE

As program administrator, the school librarian has the responsibility to choose, vet, and utilize developmentally appropriate resources for the school library. Reliability, validity, and authorship of sites are criteria used when choosing resources. The Key Commitment for Curate is to "make meaning for oneself and others by collecting, organizing, and sharing resources of personal relevance" (AASL 2018a, 94). The Competencies in the Share Domain of the *AASL Standards Framework for School Librarians* are written to establish the roles of the school librarian as teacher and information specialist to help learners work with "collaboratively constructed information sites" (AASL 2018a, School Librarian IV.C.1–3.). "Facilitating opportunities to access and evaluate collaboratively constructed information sites" can be seen in formal instructional plan choices or informal conversations about a chosen resource (AASL 2018a, School Librarian IV.C.1.). School librarians recognize, through experience, that knowing how to properly access and evaluate sites is the first step in being able to choose, vet, and utilize the available resources. Only when learners and educators know how to get to and ask critical questions about available resources will the research process be legitimate. In the context of collaboratively constructed information sites, authentically evaluating for reliability, validity, and credible authorship lends to the integrity of the chosen sites.

The Alignments in the *AASL Standards Framework for School Libraries* are written to highlight the management of the resources chosen for the school library by "establishing policies that promote effective acquisition, description, circulation, sharing, and access to resources within and beyond the school day" and by "maintaining procedures that ensure user confidentiality and promote unimpeded access to materials by staff members and learners" (AASL 2018a, School Library IV.C.3., IV.C.4.). Making these crucial management decisions establishes the school librarian and school library as authentic sources for information that are driven by integrity when making decisions.

## ENGAGE

As explained earlier, there are various questions to answer when realizing the relationship between integrity and communication. How information is gathered, used, and shared is a key component of the Engage Shared Foundation in the AASL Standards Frameworks for School Librarians and School Libraries. The roles of the school librarian as leader, teacher, and information specialist to facilitate and model ethical practices for all stakeholders when conducting research, creating products, and citing sources are emphasized in the Competencies and Alignments. "School librarians promote the responsible, ethical, and legal sharing of new information with a global community by imparting strategies for sharing information resources in accordance with modification, reuse, and remix policies" (AASL 2018a, School Librarian VI.C.1.). These strategies include the intentional thought process involved in asking why and how the information is chosen, used, and shared as a source. These same strategies reinforce integrity when communicating information to stakeholders. As the amount of information resources and formats available continues to increase, school librarians need to make all stakeholders more cognizant and deliberate in their research process.

"The school library encourages participation in a diverse learning community to create and share information by providing both online and physical spaces for the sharing and dissemination of ideas and information" (AASL 2018a, School Library VI.C.1.). When school librarians make resources available online anytime and anywhere, stakeholders can solve problems and answer questions as needed. When school librarians provide a welcoming, inclusive physical space for stakeholders, communication and connections are made with the larger community, which results in more stakeholder buy-in and support for the school library.

## Creating a Culture of Integrity

Integrity is more than truthfulness, frankness, and reliability. It is an alignment of content, energy, and consistency that is brought to every message, whether formal or informal, face-to-face or via a communication tool. There are several questions to consider about integrity and how it relates to communication. These questions include exploring how, why, where, and when integrity is important to communication and what integrity looks like in communication. School librarians realize that educators, learners, and members of the school community need the opportunity and skills to develop integrity through participating in informed conversations and debates, accessing and evaluating information sites, and utilizing specific strategies for sharing resources. When school librarians expect and model integrity as part of best practice in the school library, members of the school community also develop these same qualities in their overall communication skills. Guided by the AASL Common Beliefs, school librarians strengthen integrity by incorporating the solid values of these beliefs consistently in their communications. In addition, focusing on the Share Domain creates opportunities for the school librarian to develop and put into practice the actions that demonstrate mastery of the Competencies and Alignments from the Shared Foundations of Include, Curate, and Engage as they construct stakeholder communications embedded with integrity. As school librarians gain increasing levels of leadership and responsibility in the school environment, their integrity will assist them when they need it most. Consistent messages supported by ethical principles and foundational beliefs create a culture of integrity.

# Clarity

# 8

I t was the start of a new school year, and the district library supervisor who was serving in the roles of leader and program administrator held an opening meeting for the district school librarians. A new teacher/librarian evaluation plan was being launched with the start of the new school year. Everyone was confused, and here is why. The new PGEP was based on PQR for every HCPS LIS. And it did not stop there because the review included an OC, which included a POC. The entire presentation of twenty-two slides was loaded with acronyms and created to shorten the message. Truthfully, it was done in fun. Clearly none of the slides made any sense to those watching the presentation. Once the district library supervisor explained each acronym, along with the time line and process for observations, the yearly evaluation process became clear. Two lessons can be learned from the acronym presentation. First and foremost, clarity is impaired when messages are conveyed in a way that is ambiguous and unfamiliar to the receivers of the communication. And second, acronyms are beneficial to a limited audience. Every district, department, curriculum, and professional organization has a unique set of acronyms. In the education profession, acronyms are abundant and may lead to misunderstanding and confusion. So an important rule in communication is to limit the use of jargon and acronyms that are known only to a distinct group of people.

## Guidelines for Achieving Clarity

Clarity in communication prevents misunderstanding. It is the responsibility of the school librarian to construct communications that are designed for the audience who is receiving the information. In addition, communications should be succinct so that they direct the receiver to expected outcomes. Limiting the communication to several specific points ensures that the receiver focuses on the information that is important. Whether the communication is oral or written, clarity is required. Achieving clarity is possible when five specific guidelines are followed. These guidelines include answering the question, staying on topic, creating accurate and precise statements, using appropriate body language, and repeating the main concepts within the communication.

## *Answer the Question*

As program administrators, school librarians communicate clarifying information when questions arise about a policy or process. If a program is initiated, there may be questions about the logistics, impact, and anticipated goals of the event. Before answering any questions asked after an initial communication, a leader determines the specific details that need clarification. Many school librarians address the need to answer questions through Frequently Asked Questions (FAQs). An elementary school librarian used the rule of three when creating a FAQ communication. Drawing from the teacher role, this school librarian constructively assessed her communication after three educators asked the same question related to an announcement. This school librarian knew that three educators asking for clarification about the same point indicated confusion and necessitated clarifying the statement. When constructing answers to questions, school librarians should keep in mind that the recipients want succinct replies that target their concerns. In addition, FAQs are an opportunity to promote the positive aspects of a project. For example, a secondary school librarian was asked how a particular book was chosen for a One Book, One Community reading program because the parent asking the question felt the book contained tough subject matter. The school librarian's answer incorporated not only an outline of the book selection process but also key concepts of the principles of intellectual freedom. Part of the response included advocating that the school was a safe place where, under professional supervision, difficult topics such as the impact of alcoholism on family members could be discussed. In other cases, FAQs can educate the school community about details surrounding a library project by including program goals and objectives among the answers. School librarians who answer questions face-to-face through an open discussion gain strong support from stakeholders by resolving and clarifying concerns.

When answering questions about a communication, leaders first check that they fully understand the question before attempting to structure an answer. School librarians who use this technique have a better opportunity to clarify the issue. Leaders also make a final check for understanding to ensure that the correct meaning was interpreted by colleagues. Questions are good because they ultimately create buy-in from stakeholders, especially when the need for clarity explains how school library ideas, projects, and initiatives connect to the goals of the educational community.

## Stay on Topic

A middle school principal was very detailed and technical during faculty meetings. One afternoon the agenda for the faculty meeting included the topic of assessment. At the end of two hours, only five educators were left in the school library where the meeting was held, and the principal was still on a roll. The communication was too broad for the educators, and the information became boring and irrelevant as the principal explored one sidebar after another on the topic of assessment. This principal lost focus on the key points of the message, and the educators lost focus as well. Staying on the topic is essential for clarity. Too much information will distort and confuse the message. In this case the principal did not effectively use time. In addition, by providing so much information, he lost the attention of his audience. School librarians need to stay on topic and refrain from digressing into *interesting stories* that prevent educators from properly assimilating the information librarians are communicating.

## Use Precise Statements

When communicating, leaders use precise words and statements to create clarity in the message. *Merriam-Webster* defines *precise* as "exactly or sharply defined or stated."[1] When crafting precise messages, school librarians need to use concrete terminology that clearly explains the information. An infographic—the combination of text and graphical representations—is an ideal format that combines precise verbiage with data in charts or diagrams. Infographics are also concise tools when conveying processes. For example, a secondary school librarian created an infographic to direct learners through the research process. The infographic was posted throughout the library as a reminder of the research process and provided learners with quick and clear-cut steps to use when completing the research process.

When data are reported accurately and concisely, those receiving the message are able to assimilate the information quickly, which increases the impact of the message. In their role as program administrators, school librarians use data, reports, and research to strengthen requests for funding and resources. When school librarians communicate precise information that is clearly written and includes succinct talking points, the likelihood of successful initiation and implementation of new ideas, policies, and programs is high.

## Use Appropriate Nonverbal Communication

Body language, or nonverbal communication, impacts face-to-face interactions. It is powerful and influences how recipients view information. School librarians need to be aware that their body language includes eye movements, facial expressions, hand gestures, and posture. If body language is confident and optimistic, then the communication can be extremely positive; on the other hand, if body language is judgmental and disapproving, then the communication may be received negatively. When analyzing the use of body language, a good place to start is eye contact. Practice making eye contact with administrators, educators, and learners when listening to their comments. Maintaining eye contact is a listening skill that can then be transferred to a communication skill. Leaders realize that eye contact expresses "attentiveness, confidence, and sincerity" (Mariama-Arthur 2015). Experienced communicators know that facial expressions can sway how an audience responds to information. For example, a message's credibility is lost when the communicator grimaces to reveal displeasure during the announcement. Likewise, a smile may suggest acceptance. Using hand gestures also communicates feeling to an audience. Showing excitement by clapping or expressing victory by making a *V* with your fingers adds emphasis to communications. Posture during face-to-face meetings is telling because standing tall shows confidence and professionalism. To ensure that the communication is accepted, be proud of the message, and others will react supportively (Mariama-Arthur 2015).

## Repeat the Message

Some instructions need repeating. An elementary school librarian was giving directions to learners so that they could complete an assignment. After providing the steps to the project, she checked for understanding. One learner did not grasp the assignment, so the school librarian repeated the instructions a bit differently. Once again, the learner did not understand. At this point the school librarian asked another learner sitting beside the first learner to explain the project. Finally, the learner figured out the task that he needed to accomplish. At times, repeating messages by changing the language ensures that a communication is understood and effective. Repetition creates emphasis by focusing on important elements in a communication and provides clarity of understanding to the listener. The U.S. Army is a great illustration of what it means to repeat messages. Officers tell the troops the information they need to know, then they tell them again, and then they summarize the information, which, in essence, is telling them the message again (Garson 2017). To ensure understanding, the school librarian uses repetition when instructing learners. When sending messages as an instructional leader and program administrator, it is just as important for school librarians to repeat communications to educators.

## Define the Audience

Whether a school librarian is crafting a written message or speaking before a group of educators, decision makers, parents, or learners, clarity is critical to ensure that the communication is interpreted correctly. Every receiver of a message incorporates her own experience, vocabulary, and needs into the communication. For this reason, a leader needs to be aware of the makeup of the audience receiving the message and evaluate each communication from the perspective of the specific stakeholder to prevent misunderstandings. School librarians strive to create library directives that are inclusive and meaningful while being relevant to stakeholders. Strategies for clarity when sharing information ensure that the communication is appropriate for and accepted by the intended audience.

## Connections to the Shared Foundations

School librarians rely on clarity in order to be effective when relaying information to stakeholders. When school librarians are deliberate in crafting directions and messages, depending on the intended stakeholder, the outcome is more successful. School librarians practice and strengthen their clarity skills when they model those skills to learners during formal directions and informal conversations. Modeling clarity affects learners' and stakeholders' attitudes toward how they, in turn, convey messages. The AASL Standards Frameworks for School Librarians and School Libraries reinforce this idea with Competencies and Alignments in the Share Domain that foster school librarians taking an active role in facilitating opportunities to develop clarity for themselves and their stakeholders. The Shared Foundations of Include, Curate, and Engage specifically address contributing to discussions or sites and sharing information in a global community.

### INCLUDE

When discussions consist of many viewpoints, the hope is that the ideas being exchanged become more thoughtful and richer for the participants. Unfortunately, the opposite can happen, and chaos can break out if the participants are not clear in presenting their ideas. "School librarians facilitate experiences in which learners exhibit empathy and tolerance for diverse ideas by guiding learners to contribute to discussions in which multiple viewpoints on a topic are expressed" (AASL 2018a, School Librarian II.C.2.). When learners identify what clarity is and practice using clarity in communication in a structured, safe environment such as the school library, they are able to develop the skill to apply to other discussions outside school.

At the elementary level, an experience for learners could be Generous Genres, a lunchtime group that meets to discuss different examples of books within a given genre each month. Because people have various reactions to books, guiding learners to be clear and specific in why they like or dislike a book will empower them to participate effectively in the discussion and be listened to by peers. The guidance by the school librarian could include asking clarifying questions or having learners write down their ideas before speaking. This practice will help the learners as they grow older to be more comfortable in discussing chosen books with other people.

Secondary-level learners often come to the school library to research information for persuasive papers. When learners find out they are writing a persuasive paper, the first lesson is to explain that the issue they chose is what they are advocating. For example, if their position is to defend the cons of online learning, they must clearly embrace and defend that position. As an opener to a persuasive paper writing assignment, the school librarian might ask the class to stand in a straight line in the middle of the library. Then the librarian could invite all those who like a particular soft drink to take a step to the right and all those who like a competing soft drink brand to take a step to the left. There will always be learners still standing in the middle who will complain that they do not like either choice. In a persuasive paper there is no middle ground, and learners must pick a position and defend it with convincing evidence and key points. The most effective persuasive papers are written by learners who understand the view opposite the one they are defending. Persuasive papers require logic and reason and must differentiate between fact and fiction. Data are important to defending the point of view. As learners research and collect information about their topic, they become more understanding of diverse views and more aware of their own biases.

The chaos or frustration occurring in discussions because participants are not clear in their message also arises during the collaborative process when school librarians interact with classroom educators as instructional partners. School librarians need to be clear in their intended instructional goals and proposed assessments when working with classroom educators in order to maintain the need for the school library and school librarian in the overall research process. Creating a graphic organizer or an online document that lists the instructional goals and available resources in well-thought-out, deliberate plans will help avoid miscommunications and will make the lesson more successful for everyone involved.

The school librarian also realizes how the school library functions as a part of the larger school community. "The school library facilitates opportunities to experience diverse ideas by implementing solutions that address physical, social, cultural, linguistic, and intellectual barriers to equitable access to resources and services" (AASL 2018a, School Library II.C.1.). Are both nonfiction information and literary resources available? Which digital and print formats of resources are available? How accessible are the resources through technology? Are the different cultural populations being represented and are needs being met by the resources? Are the resources developmentally appropriate? All these questions must be asked by the school librarian, fulfilling the roles of information specialist and program administrator, in order to use the resources as solutions for and connectors to the larger school community. These questions also need to be clearly answered and supported by data for the administrators, at the building and district levels, to justify using the resources chosen as solutions for the larger community.

## CURATE

In choosing information sites, learners have a multitude of options today because of the increase in social media and collaboratively constructed sites such as Wikipedia. Teaching learners, including fellow educators, how to use clarity when contributing to collaboratively constructed sites and how to ethically use others' work is the responsibility of the school librarian as teacher, instructional partner, and information specialist. Using clarity when contributing to collaborative information sites is crucial because other people can access, read, and use the information any way they want. "School librarians contribute to and guide information resource exchange within and beyond the school learning community by devising pathways for learners to contribute to collaboratively constructed information sites by ethically using and reproducing others' work" (AASL 2018a, School Librarian IV.C.2.). These pathways can be both abstract and concrete and can help to broaden learners' and educators' thinking.

One example of a concrete pathway is the opportunity for learners and educators to include research writing activities that develop clear, vetted, written messages based on data in lessons. Choosing topics based on interest and finding data to support a thesis statement about the chosen topic encourage learners to articulate and share their ideas. The educator benefits from the ability of learners to choose based on interest because it makes the learners more invested in the research process and implementation of the whole lesson. The guidance facilitated by school librarians could start with learners spending time in the school library designing the messages and using researched data in different formats to support the ideas. The messages could be designed as public service announcements to be displayed through a collaboratively constructed site for the entire school. Guiding the learners to be clear and concise in the message will boost the strength of the message. This experience encourages both learners and educators to be articulate when communicating their ideas.

Another example of a concrete pathway is the modeling of ethical access to and use of collaboratively constructed sites. An elementary school librarian used the Book Creator app with second graders in the school library to create and showcase their fiction stories and offer the opportunity to collaborate with other learners. Because Book Creator is a collaboratively constructed site, the school librarian was intentional in her modeling of how to review others' work respectfully and seek permission from the other learner before adding to a story. This lesson was then extended to the classroom after the school librarian, as information specialist, taught the classroom educator how to use Book Creator and continue the creative process in the classroom. The learners' creativity thrived when they were given the opportunity to use Book Creator in both spaces, and the classroom educator was given another tool to use.

Examples of abstract pathways include informal discussions and conversations about information being shared on collaboratively constructed sites, planting the seeds of critically thinking about what information is being shared. Through discussions and asking clarifying questions, school librarians and learners have the opportunity to process the information found and respond or contribute information with clarity. This auditory processing of information serves as a base for creating communication skills that extend beyond the immediate conversations.

As program administrator, the school librarian must be accountable to building- and district-level administrators in order to receive full support and credibility. One way to show accountability is by "including and tracking collection materials in a system that uses standardized approaches to description and location [of information]" (AASL 2018a, School Library IV.C.1.). Although in some localities, this system of tracking materials may be district-wide, it is the building-level school librarian's responsibility to understand the statistics and realize how to use the data to further the school library. For example, when the daily circulation statistics and number of classes taught exceed the number of support staff available, the school librarian can use the data to advocate for more support staff time or funding.

## ENGAGE

The ethical sharing of information has become a global issue and one that people need to be intentionally taught how to do correctly. With the increase in social media and people becoming less mindful of using clarity in communications, having specific policies in place becomes more important. The school librarian, through the roles of information specialist and leader, takes this responsibility seriously when serving as a resource person for the larger school community. "School librarians promote the responsible, ethical, and legal sharing of new information with a global community by imparting strategies for sharing information resources in accordance with modification, reuse, and remix policies" (AASL 2018a, School Librarian VI.C.1.). These strategies include posting the policies in the school library for all stakeholders to see, modeling how to access and use reliable citation tools for learners and educators, and deliberately integrating the citation step into the research process. The more learners are exposed to and adhere to the citation policies, the more comfortable they will become incorporating this step into their research process.

"Providing a context in which the school librarian can model for learners, other educators, and administrators multiple strategies to locate, evaluate, and ethically use information for specific purposes" is one of the main functions of a school library (AASL 2018a, School Library VI.C.2.). Initiating, designing, and implementing strong professional development for educators and administrators, both within a specific school and district-wide, is one way that school libraries can guarantee the strategies being incorporated into the larger school environment.

## Facilitating Clarity

Clarity is delivering information that is well thought out and without ambiguity. To be effective, the message must be relevant to the user. Achieving clarity when communicating is possible when school librarians follow guidelines that include answering the question, staying on topic, creating accurate and precise statements, using appropriate body language, and repeating the main concepts of the message. The clarity of professional oral and written communications is strengthened when the school librarian uses these techniques to compose information statements and announcements for stakeholders. In addition, the accuracy of the message provides a clear direction for the recipients and avoids misunderstandings. Using the *AASL Standards Framework for School Librarians* as a guide, school librarians realize that the development of communication skills is crucial to learners' success. As they teach learners the Competencies from the Shared Foundations of Include, Curate, and Engage in the Share Domain, school librarians focus on providing opportunities for learners to show tolerance through discussions, ethically create and share information globally, and develop clear messages to be more effective. School librarians must practice clarity when teaching learners, but they must also refine their own skills by deliberately and intentionally crafting understandable, informative communications for educators, parents, and the school community.

**NOTE**

1. https://www.merriam-webster.com/dictionary/precise

# Delivery Methods

# 9

Every evening Abby, the dog, went for one last visit outside before sleeping through the night. On one particular evening she disappeared into the blackness. When the owners called for her, Abby was not to be found. Soliciting the help of others, friends circled the house calling Abby by name. No response. Finally, she was discovered under a streetlight in the middle of a side street. It took this event for her owners to realize that the aging Abby was deaf. From that point onward when Abby went out at night, she wore a lighted collar. In addition, the owners started communicating with Abby through hand motions, training her on essential commands such as "come," "stay," and "walk." Abby needed a different communication style to keep her safe. Most of our audiences need some form of communication accommodation as well.

Differentiated communication by school librarians to learners, educators, and the school community creates successful understanding of the information disseminated in school library communications. Part of a blueprint for delivering communications is exploring varied methods of communication and matching them with the unique qualities of each stakeholder. Creating a communication plan before sending out communiques increases the opportunity for comprehension of the messages' meaning. Understanding the experiences and needs of learners, educators, and community members helps in framing messages in a language that the receiver is familiar with.

## Communicating with Stakeholders

The *National School Library Standards for Learners, School Librarians, and School Libraries* introduces personas as a way for school librarians to more effectively connect with stakeholders and bring the AASL Standards to life. Referring to these personas is a way to identify with school library stakeholders and understand their "wants, needs, and motivations" (AASL 2018a, 20). These personas have defined profiles at https://standards.aasl.org/project/personas, which also provides ideas for connecting each stakeholder to the AASL Standards. In addition, the personas list information important to each stakeholder, which creates an opportunity to customize messages that need to be delivered. There are exceptions to personas developed in the AASL Standards. For example, student learners, community members, and business leaders are not defined with a persona profile. As a result, school librarians may consider modifying or creating new personas as needed as they evaluate the groups they collaborate with in their own communities. The personas provided can be anchor points when school librarians are not sure how to proceed with communication of information to a particular group.

### Connecting to Learners

"The standards included in the *AASL Standards Framework for Learners* acknowledge that people are learners throughout their lives" (AASL 2018a, 28). When implementing differentiated communications, it is important to recognize that connecting to learners in Pre-K–12 must be in a delivery format that they are familiar with and value. As with all learners, it is important to know that Pre-K–12 learners' prior knowledge influences their level of acceptance of new information. Learners engage with new knowledge after following a research process and then use the new knowledge collaboratively. By "giving learners opportunities to engage in informed conversation and active debate," school librarians help learners to internalize the information (AASL 2018aa, School Librarian II.C.I.). Using this process in the instructional environment creates deep understanding as learners consume new information and interpret new knowledge. The Shared Foundation Curate reminds us that "school librarians contribute to and guide information resource exchange within and beyond the school learning community by directing learners to join others to compare and contrast information derived from collaboratively constructed information sites" (AASL 2018a, School Librarian IV.C.3.). It is from this collaborative experience that learners derive meaning. Therefore, as teacher, the school librarian should instruct early learners by incorporating these curation processes to enhance learners' assimilation of instructional and other communications.

### Connecting to Classroom Educators

The persona of Tony the Teacher, as described in the *National School Library Standards for Learners, School Librarians, and School Libraries,* reminds school librarians to consider how many years Tony has been in his current position. Also, the online profile explores Tony's professional qualifications, including his leadership roles, technology experience, and current library/AASL connections. The exciting part of the online profiles is specific connections to the AASL Standards with a rationale identifying what Tony understands or needs as an educator. Tony is a great example to use when crafting and delivering a message to educators; however, take time to customize this educator to the unique situation in your school. Under the Domain Think, educators may question the introduction of a new tool for research. Like Tony, they may ask, what demands will this tool place on my time? How does it support my own curriculum? What might the school librarian contribute to teaching and learning in my classroom? Addressing these concerns within a communication enables Tony the Teacher to understand how this new tool and the library will be useful to him (AASL 2018b).

### Connecting to Administrators

When working with school administrators, school librarians can gain insight and tips for communicating with decision makers from Leon the Lead Learner. School librarians are advised of the goals of an administrator through reading about Leon. For example, he wants to know what he can learn from his school librarian about technology, literacy, and his school. He would like to know how the school library can advance the learning culture of the school. Leon also wants to know how the library can serve as a center for equitable access to learning opportunities. Each of these statements is well worded and targets most administrator needs. When the school librarian infuses these concepts into everyday communications, administrators find answers to their needs. Leon's persona profile shows that technology is an important part of his professional life. It is important for school librarians to key into their individual administrator's passion when providing a rationale for school library initiatives (AASL 2018b).

### Connecting to Parents

Communications to parents or guardians are assisted by referring to the persona of Patty the Parent. The information in the Domain Create under the persona of Patty the Parent provides ideas for how to best communicate to parents in the school community. The persona reminds school librarians that parents want to be included as stakeholders *and* users. The persona suggests

that a variety of delivery modes, including infographics, flyers, videos, and social media, is important so that Patty the Parent understands the information. Consider using multiple delivery modes to reach out to parents and other stakeholders outside the walls of the school. Developing rapport with the community creates relationships that are reciprocal. It is the beginning of engaging parents in future advocacy efforts as well as opening a communication pathway (AASL 2018b).

## Delivering the Message

Knowing your audience's needs and experiences is the first step in two-way communication. Next, choosing a delivery method that uses the professional writing, speaking, and listening skills of a school librarian must be considered. Several options to examine when developing a plan for delivering the message are face-to-face, social media, written communications, and conference calls. Although each option is beneficial for distributing messages, one method may be more effective than another depending on the content of the information.

### Face-to-Face

In the AASL *National School Library Standards for Learners, School Librarians, and School Libraries,* the Shared Foundation of Include encourages school librarians to facilitate "opportunities to engage in informed conversation and active debate" (AASL 2018a, School Librarian II.C.1.). When communicating to stakeholders, the acceptance of diverse ideas broadens and deepens understanding. Facilitating an open conversation includes organizing stakeholder groups for decision making and problem solving where they can engage with others and where the school librarian as teacher models respect for multiple viewpoints (AASL 2018a, School Librarian II.C.2.). These foundational Competencies illustrate elements that are important in face-to-face communication. Whether the face-to-face interaction is with an individual, a group, or an organization, it is best used when interactive discussion is important to the information being delivered.

In the digital environment of the school, in which communication via e-mail and social media is instantaneous, face-to-face communication has some advantages. One such advantage is that body language indicates whether the message is accepted or not. It shows immediately whether the group receiving the message is engaged or distracted. School librarians as leaders know that face-to-face communication eliminates back-and-forth e-mail messages that question some aspect of the message because it allows for discussion surrounding uncertainty to take place at the time the information is delivered. In this sense, face-to-face communication may be more efficient. When school librarians are looking for creative input into a situation, a face-to-face meeting allows for group interaction and brainstorming. This collaboration builds a sense of community as participants interact and social-ize during the gathering ("The Importance of Face-to-Face Communication" 2013).

A good guideline for school librarians is to use face-to-face communication when collaboration and inclusion are needed. It is also important to use an open meeting format when "information must be disseminated to every member of the organization. Having one large meeting saves time and assures that the same mes-sage is heard by all. In situations in which new initiatives, policies, or procedures are shared, large meetings allow all to hear the conversation, questions, and concerns" (Martin 2013, 72).

When a face-to-face meeting with everyone in the same room is not realistic, online meeting rooms can create a similar sense of community. Improved connec-tivity and technology in schools make online meeting rooms effective and inter-active. This face-to-face meeting requires a computer, Internet connectivity, and web conferencing software. Some web conferencing software is fee-based, but good software is available for free as well. A group of five district library supervisors who lived in three different time zones met monthly through an online meeting room. They shared best practices and provided support when issues surfaced for which they needed guidance from each other. In the past, meeting face-to-face with edu-cators in different time zones and living miles apart would not have been possi-ble. The newest selection of online meeting rooms provides easy access and is used when the value of personal contact is important, particularly for educators who are separated by distance or are located in remote situations.

## Social Media

Social media change the way communication is delivered, create opportunities for advocacy, and promote content to educators and the greater community. A study from the Pew Research Center showed that social media users log into their accounts at least once a day and that many check their accounts multiple times a day (Newberry 2018). Knowing the potential behind social media makes it a powerful choice when creating interest in the school library. "Consider that there are now more than 3 bil-lion using social networks across the globe" (Newberry 2018). The intended audience governs which social media tool to choose for the greatest impact.

The advantages of social media have grown since different platforms first launched. As more learners, educators, and members of the school community engage with the school library through social media, the expanding audience enhances the relevance and outreach of information. Two-way communication encourages expressing views that provide the school librarian with reactions to news as well as an opportunity for the school librarian to address comments provided by users. Learners may post a picture or chat about information from an event that is taking place in the library. Most media outlets are capitalizing on "trending" stories and clips that are available on social media. School librarians can use "trending" news to connect learners with science, technology, sports, and other news. Another benefit of social media is the ability to post live events and activities. For example, social media can be used to launch an author event. Social media continue to change, offering a wide range of communication options to school librarians.

When delivering advocacy messages, social media are quick and effective. At a district-wide school library meeting, it was announced that multiple school libraries had just been chosen to receive thousands of dollars of grant funding to purchase books. The initial announcement was to be kept secret until a national press release was issued several days later, but the school librarians were not told this. As the good news was being announced by the foundation's representative, many of the recipients began sharing the information on social media. Immediately, the representative stopped and asked the school librarians to wait until the official press release. In an instant the news was spreading. The timeliness of social media needs to be assessed when using that form of communication. School librarians need to be aware of the immediacy of messages being communicated through social media. Depending on the information to be shared, social media may not be the best way to reach out to stakeholders.

Promoting content to educators and the community is informative, fun, and interactive. The important aspect of sharing content through social media is the communication of useful information to the community. Perhaps a seasonal library event is being planned, or perhaps extended library lending periods are being instituted. A district school library supervisor used an infographic to communicate her quarterly report on social media. The report provided data on how the school librarians were growing lifelong readers and transforming learners. Data included 449,000+ learners reached, 6,550 interlibrary loans, 442,121 books circulated, 11,630+ classes taught, and 8,000+ staff consultations and collaborations (HCPS 2018a). These numbers are powerful, and the graphic provided links to further information. Social media provide avenues for pictures and videos as well as links to the library. When posting to a social media platform, the school librarian needs to ensure that the value of the school library is being expressed to stakeholders and that the information is relevant to the readers.

## Written Communication

E-mail, newsletters, infographics, program proposals, manuals, and just about anything that needs to be shared in a written format requires a set of skills to make the communication effective. The writing must be logical, sequential, and brief and have proper spelling, grammar, and punctuation. The focus and objectives of the message must be clear and written in a style that the learners and educators understand. The benefits of written communication are that it provides a record of shared information, can summarize processes, prevents distortion of the information, and can circulate easily. In addition, written communication can be transmitted at a time that makes the greatest impact.

E-mail is a quick method of sending information to educators and community members. School librarians need to review each e-mail before sending it to other educators and community members to make sure that the key message is understandable. "In the name of speed, we throw caution to the winds and forget sentence patterning, paragraphing, and other conventions that make messages intelligible, creating unattractive and impenetrable data dumps. Given this unfortunate trend, many business experts counsel companies to install firm guidelines on tone, content, and shape of e-mail correspondence" ("Written Communication," n.d.). Because it is hard, if not impossible, to take back mistakes, school librarians should ask a trusted educator to review important e-mail communications. "The benefit of e-mail is that it provides a date stamp, creating a record of when information was shared. The message reaches all members of the organization at approximately the same time. When the message has little or no emotional component, an e-mail is the most convenient choice" (Martin 2013, 72).

Newsletters and infographics can be delivered by digital means or in a printed format. Consider designing a template that attracts readers to the school library story. Brevity is also effective for these two methods of communicating information and helps the stakeholder enjoy content without getting bogged down in too many details. To keep learners, educators, and parents coming back to read future newsletters and infographics, think about sharing data or an idea for a program that surprises them. Infographics need data that are relevant to the reader. Any pictures and links to further information need captions that explain, and guide stakeholders to understand, the power of the school library for learners. With digital messages, consider offering interactive elements such as surveys and emojis for readers to provide feedback.

School librarians as leaders know that program proposals need to include basic information, such as goals, objectives, and a time line. A proposal, whether it is for additional resources or a program event, should have a written component for the administration to review. Once the administration approves the idea, it is important to present the proposal to the school leadership committee. School librarians who identify and then use the organizational structure of the school community often gain widespread acceptance and support for proposals.

Manuals are critical to organizational consistency. A library manual contains policies and procedures that guide library operations. One school district made the library organizational manual digital, thus creating a living document that could be constantly updated. Online manuals are easier to revise, providing quicker communication of policies and procedures. The district library supervisor made sure that when information was added or changed, the section of the manual with the new information was highlighted with green and linked to the table of contents. After several months the highlighted section changed to yellow, and after two more months the highlighting was removed. The highlighting drew school librarians to important changes. In addition, an e-mail was generated to all educators impacted by the information change.

### Conference Calls

Conference calls provide an opportunity for school librarians to complete work in a time-efficient manner. The ease of having the participants just pick up a phone makes conference calling attractive. Technology and the Internet are not stumbling blocks when using conference calls to complete collaborative committee work and problem solve. Some basic protocols should be followed when conference calls are chosen as a means of communication. As with any meeting, an agenda should be provided and then followed during the call. Because no visual is available, it is critical that all respondents identify themselves every time they speak. This protocol is nonnegotiable and is necessary so that all members of the conference call know who is providing the information. It is also important to have a time limit on how long participants talk because there is no way to provide a physical clue to someone who is on a tangent. Therefore, prior to a call, make sure all participants know that they are limited to a set number of minutes, after which they must give another participant an opportunity to comment. Mute the phone when listening to others to avoid distracting noises. As with any meeting, conference calls need a leader who makes sure the logistics are sent out to participants ahead of time. This same leader guides the participants through the agenda during the call (Bennett 2013).

## Connecting to the Shared Foundations

Choosing which delivery method to use to relay messages is part of learning to communicate effectively. For school librarians, the effectiveness of the message can affect the buy-in from stakeholders and result in positive or negative changes for the school library. The Share Domain in the AASL Standards Frameworks for School Librarians and School Libraries reinforces the importance of choosing delivery methods by emphasizing the "importance of the school librarian's encouraging learners to responsibly share their innovative solutions to problems in multiple formats to appropriate audiences" (AASL 2018a, 45). Although the Shared Foundations of Include, Curate, and Engage list Competencies and Alignments that identify school librarians' role in teaching learners to contribute to and share information, school librarians realize the importance of reaching the highest performance level of the Competencies themselves to maximize the potential of the school library.

## INCLUDE

"School librarians facilitate experiences in which learners exhibit empathy and tolerance for diverse ideas by giving learners opportunities to engage in informed conversation and active debate" (AASL 2018a, School Librarian II.C.1.). When the school librarian nurtures productive debate and conversations, ideally learners feel safe to express their authentic ideas while being open to others' ideas. These informed conversations and active debates, whether intentionally designed or spontaneous, cultivate communication skills, which make the stakeholders more invested in the school library. The choice of formats to document these conversations and debates is pertinent to the comfort level of the stakeholders and provides the opportunity for conversations to continue at a later time.

For the school librarian, the role of instructional partner is vital to the success of the school library. This idea is supported through the *AASL Standards Framework for School Libraries:* "The school library facilitates opportunities to experience diverse ideas by constructing a learning environment that fosters the sharing of a wide range of viewpoints and ideas" (AASL 2018a, School Library II.C.3.). The school librarian understands that this learning environment is extended beyond the school library into meetings with classroom educators because effectively communicating and collaborating with classroom educators results in interactive, curriculum-based lessons for the learners. The delivery methods chosen to communicate with classroom educators affect the level of respect and support. An elementary-level school librarian realized the need to use different delivery methods to make connections with the fourth-grade educators. The first format she used was an e-mail to the grade-level chair about attending the grade-level weekly meeting to talk about upcoming curriculum and propose a new idea for a level-wide reading program. The second format she used was the face-to-face meeting. When the school librarian sat down at the table with the educators, the first thing she said was, "How can I help you?" This simple question made the educators pause for a moment and then take a few minutes to talk about some stressors that were impeding their ability to focus. After they were finished talking, the school librarian brought up the new reading program idea and the reasoning for needing a new grade-level-wide reading program. The teachers were open to the idea, asking clarifying questions and tweaking the guidelines with the school librarian. After the collaborative process, the school librarian followed up with an e-mail to the educators thanking them for allowing her the time to visit the meeting and providing detailed plans of the reading program. The use of appropriate communication formats and the empathy shown made the collaborative process effective and contributed to the educators' belief in the value of the school library.

## CURATE

Because more collaboratively constructed sites are available now, learning to contribute to and compare information for legitimacy on these sites become critical life skills to develop. "School librarians contribute to and guide information resource exchange within and beyond the school learning community by directing learners to join others to compare and contrast information derived from collaboratively constructed information sites" (AASL 2018a, School Librarian IV.C.3.). Because school librarians realize the importance of comparing and contrasting information between sites to vet for legitimacy, reliability, and credibility, this practice becomes an intentional part of a school librarian's lesson, giving learners practice within the school library environment. When learners are empowered and supported to compare and contrast with others, they can authentically use information from collaboratively constructed sites in an effective manner. The use of information in deliberate and reflective ways to make meaning fosters learners' wanting to share resources of personal relevance with others through social media formats.

When stakeholders such as classroom educators, administrators, and learners are invested in the school library, they feel empowered to be involved in the decision making that affects the school library. The *AASL Standards Framework for School Libraries* supports this idea by emphasizing the roles of the school librarian as leader and program administrator in creating opportunities for stakeholders to become involved in the school library. "The school library facilitates the contribution and exchange of information within and among learning communities by providing an environment in which resources that support the school's curriculum and learning goals can be collaboratively selected and developed" (AASL 2018a, School Library IV.C.1.). This collaboration for selection can be as simple as creating an online form for learners to submit ideas for new literature purchases or an online document to share with the classroom educators and building-level administrators for curriculum-based resource selections. More involved would be creating an advisory board to meet face-to-face intermittently to discuss selection ideas. Decisions made by the school librarian thus depend on the larger learning community and meeting its needs best.

## ENGAGE

The choice of delivery methods to publish information depends on the intended audience. Being safe, legal, and ethical when sharing information is the emphasis of the Engage Shared Foundation. "School librarians promote the responsible, ethical, and legal sharing of new information with a global community by guiding the dissemination of new knowledge through means appropriate for the intended audience" (AASL 2018a, School Librarian VI.C.2.). As information specialists in their school, school librarians disseminate information to many different audiences, both internally and externally, for various purposes. Being intentional in identifying the intended audience and choosing what is developmentally appropriate for the audience are critical steps in the thought process before sharing information. Modeling is the most effective way for school librarians to show stakeholders evidence of the thought processes involved in deciding how to share new knowledge. Such modeling can range from sharing exciting school library news or products through Twitter or the district-level communications department to posting products on a format whereby parents can view school library lessons.

"The school library encourages participation in a diverse learning community to create and share information by providing both online and physical spaces for the sharing and dissemination of ideas and information" (AASL 2018a, School Library VI.C.1.). Making sure these online and physical spaces are readily accessible and easy to navigate ensures that the stakeholders' communication needs are being met. All stakeholders need to feel welcome and supported by the school librarian and the school library in order for the school library to become an accepted and integral part of the larger school community.

## Creating a Blueprint for Effective Communication

Delivery methods have a strong influence on whether a message is communicated effectively or not. Depending on the intended audience, the delivery method chosen can be appropriate or it can make the message unclear. Whether school librarians choose face-to-face meetings, social media, or conference calls when delivering messages, they must use written skills that are professional. Before crafting the message, school librarians must also understand who they are communicating to by analyzing which stakeholder will receive the communication. Using the personas developed in the AASL Standards provides insight into the various stakeholders' experiences, needs, and motivations. Incorporating the Competencies and Alignments in the Share Domain for Include, Curate, and Engage into the school librarian's lessons and personal practice allows the school librarian as well as learners and educators to master how to authentically communicate in different ways. From exhibiting tolerance during informed conversations and active debates to ethically contributing to collaboratively constructed sites to sharing information with the larger global community, school librarians as well as their learners and fellow educators develop life-ready skills that are applicable to their overall lives. School librarians realize the potential of the school library to develop these skills using the AASL Standards Frameworks for School Librarians and School Libraries. Stakeholders benefit when the school librarian intentionally designs communication opportunities based on the Competencies and Alignments in the Shared Foundations. Building effective communication to stakeholders is a blueprint for successful libraries.

**PART C: COMMUNICATION**

## Reflection Questions

Provide thoughtful answers to the following reflection questions using the lines provided.

How does providing educators opportunities to engage in informed conversations and active debates strengthen the integrity of your communication skills?

_____

_____

Why is it important for you to achieve clarity when communicating?

_____

_____

What type of information will you decide to share by using an infographic? Why?

_____

_____

How are integrity, clarity, and delivery methods interrelated to provide effective communications?

_____

_____

What other Shared Foundations, Domains, and Competencies and Alignments in the AASL Standards Frameworks for School Librarians and School Libraries could you apply to integrity, clarity, and delivery format when communicating? Explain how.

_____

_____

_____

## Self-Assessment

**Goal:** To self-assess and take action on my communications objectives

A number 1 choice indicates a need for growth, a number 2 choice indicates areas to observe for more consistency, and a number 3 choice indicates the objective is accomplished.

### STRENGTHENING INTEGRITY

| | | |
|---|---|---|
| | **3.** | I always align my personal beliefs with AASL Common Beliefs before communicating. |
| | **2.** | I usually align my personal beliefs with AASL Common Beliefs before communicating. |
| | **1.** | I have difficulty aligning my personal beliefs with AASL Common Beliefs before communicating. |

### STRENGTHENING INTEGRITY

| | | |
|---|---|---|
| | **3.** | I always allow differing viewpoints to be voiced in a safe environment. |
| | **2.** | I usually allow differing viewpoints to be voiced in a safe environment. |
| | **1.** | I have difficulty allowing differing viewpoints to be voiced when communicating. |

### PROMOTING CLARITY

| | | |
|---|---|---|
| | **3.** | I always develop succinct communications that direct the receiver to expected outcomes. I communicate using precise words and statements. |
| | **2.** | I usually develop succinct communications that direct the receiver to expected outcomes. I usually communicate using precise words and statements. |
| | **1.** | I have difficulty developing succinct communications that direct the receiver to expected outcomes. I rarely communicate using precise words and statements. |

### DELIVERING COMMUNICATIONS

| | | |
|---|---|---|
| | **3.** | I always analyze learners', educators', and community members' experiences and needs when framing messages. |
| | **2.** | I usually analyze learners', educators', and community members' experiences and needs when framing messages. |
| | **1.** | I have difficulty analyzing learners', educators', and community members' experiences and needs when framing messages. |

## Breakthrough Skills

There are three professional growth breakthroughs to focus on that connect to integrity, clarity, and delivery methods that facilitate communication. These skills are to be authentic, ask yourself questions, and get feedback. Each of these skills contributes to making effective decisions that strengthen both the intent and content of the message.

- **Be authentic** in your choices. Communication is only effective when the receiver feels that the message and the delivery method are authentic. The culture of integrity is developed when the message is authentic for the receiver. Being intentional and authentic when communicating will benefit the school librarian's credibility as well as the school library's position in the larger school community and among its stakeholders.

- **Ask yourself questions** about the thought process involved in communication. How are integrity, clarity, and the delivery method connected, shown, and supported in my proposed communication? What is my purpose for communicating with this person? Why am I reaching out or giving information to this person? Being mindful and asking questions throughout the communication process will result in clearer messages and better decisions.

- **Get feedback** on the proposed communication. Use the AASL personas or role-play to test the effectiveness of the communication. Practice self-assessment to reflect on decisions concerning integrity, clarity, and the chosen delivery method. Ask others to give feedback on how the message was received and whether the communication was practical for its purpose, resulting in better communication the next time.

# Relationship Building

B uilding strong relationships that are positive, supportive, and recip-rocal provides benefits to the school librarian and the school library. Growth in leadership skills as it relates to relationship building requires fostering ideas and concepts within the school library that emphasize inclusion, collaboration, and engagement. Strengthen these skills and a valued workplace environment is developed. Relationship building is not new, but there are several considerations to explore when relationships are nurtured to gain school library support. For example, relationships in a digital age are developed instantly and yet, because of the lack of face-to-face interaction, they are often short-lived. As a result, school librarians must be more deliberate and prioritize how to use digital connections to enhance interactions. Creating focused support for the school library is dependent on collaboration that results in shared goals. Leaders cultivate relationships up, down, and sideways in their organization. Each of the five roles of a school librarian provides leadership opportunities to influence different segments of the school community. The school librarian builds relationships with and among varied stakeholders by forming strategic partnerships. These partnerships rely on developing a culture of self-awareness and promoting empowerment by increasing stakeholders' level of responsibility in the school library. Respect for learners, educators, and parents is advanced by "creating and maintaining a learning environment that supports and stimulates discussion from all members of the school community" (AASL 2018a, School Library III.D.1.). This approach gets everyone involved and supportive of a positive learning environment. School librarians create self-awareness by "showcasing learners' reflections on their place within the global learning community" (AASL 2018a, School Librarian II.D.3.). It is through partnerships, self-awareness, and empowerment that school librarians develop the relationships needed to prompt positive results for the school library.

## A Relationship-Building Challenge for School Librarians

Part of relationship building includes meeting the demands of various demographics in the school. This aspect of relationship building includes the cultural and economic diversity within the school library and in the overall school instructional setting. The varied demographics found in today's schools impact selection of resources, building of relationships, and overall teaching. Managing the school library to meet diversity is challenging. With emphasis on the global learning community, school librarians ensure that information and ideas are located in a diverse collection (AASL 2018a, School Library II.D.1.). Varied demographics also impact partnerships that are dependent on the ability of learners and educators to develop empathy for the cultural and economic differences that often threaten to segment the school community. When building relationships, the Competencies in the Grow Domain from the *AASL Standards Framework for School Librarians* and the Alignments for School Libraries provide opportunities for librarians to model and develop relationship-building skills by practicing and applying the Shared Foundations of Include, Collaborate, and Engage. Knowing these skills is one thing, but applying them is the key! As leaders, school librarians must meet the diversity challenge by tapping into the unique traditions of their learners, educators, and parents to empower change.

# 10

# Partnerships

Partnerships in education are powerful alliances among groups within the school, district, state, and nation where purposeful cooperation benefits learners and educators. The school librarian is instrumental in developing multidimensional partnerships because librarians fulfill five roles within the school. School librarians are leaders, instructional partners, information specialists, teachers, and program administrators. Each of the five interconnected roles provides powerful connections to stakeholders when making decisions, supporting accountability, stimulating innovation, and increasing academic growth. Partnerships create shared responsibility and cooperation for school library initiatives.

The school librarian knows that there are strategies that foster partnerships, beginning with making each partnership reciprocal and complementary. School librarians develop practices that increase effective relationship building because partnerships are important for achieving school library goals. The partnerships promote shared responsibility by effectively utilizing individual strengths. The school librarian uses daily interactions to build layers of stakeholder relationships. Partnerships require emotional and physical investments to maximize results. Emotional investment requires being open to ideas, flexible in how stakeholders work together, and reliable for follow-through. Physical investments in forming partnerships are time and money, such as for operating book fairs, providing library apps, and constructing access to databases.

## Importance of Partnerships

Partnerships provide a competitive edge for school library projects by increasing the resources available to achieve daily objectives and accomplish new goals.

Tapping into the expertise of members of the school community, whether they be learners, educators, administrators, or community members, increases the skill set available to the school librarian and provides unique perspectives when fulfilling library needs. For example, when a new secondary school was being built, the start-up principal gathered a team of department chairs and the school librarian a year before the school was to open. The principal wanted a "smart technology" school, starting with the infrastructure, the devices, and the curriculum. A parent who worked in information technology for a major corporation offered to assist with the infrastructure and technology. The principal made the parent a member of the start-up team. This parent's insight into large networks, vendor compliance, and computer language made a difference in how the team focused on technology plans. The parent's expertise provided confidence and direction for what was possible to achieve. The team members' vision for instruction expanded as a result of the parent's knowledge about flexible options for delivering varied technology. The school librarian's knowledge of cloud computing assisted the team by bringing up questions about security, maintenance expenses, and future capacity for the network. In addition, the school librarian's deep understanding of the integration of technology with teaching and learning provided insight into the purchase of databases and programming grounded in the pedagogical needs of learners. By serving on this team, the school librarian ensured that the library was built with adequate technology, learning spaces, and resources to support learners, educators, and the community. This start-up team formed a partnership that extended way beyond opening day. The school became a model for cross-curricular learning. For example, the science classes came to the school library to research the physics of bridges. The learners' research papers were then graded for grammar by the English educators while the science educators reviewed the papers for content. From its opening day, this school with a technology-driven environment was a success. The partnership among curriculum leaders, the school librarian, administration, and the community made a difference.

With increased digital opportunities, school librarians must maintain relevance to prove the school library's value. Even though school libraries promote academic inquiry, provide cultural connections to diverse populations, and provide equity across economic levels, sometimes this message does not get out to the public. When school librarians encourage community members to become involved with the school library, the silence of success is transformed into noisy expressions of excitement. Partnerships also build a history of accomplishment that feeds into recognition for the library, the school, and the district.

## Meeting Economic Needs

Economic downturns often create a funding battle in the school environment because there are limited funds available and many competing needs. The school librarian creates a culture of abundance by extending resources from the library across the school and into the homes of learners and educators. School librarians have a global knowledge of curriculum and student pedagogy enabling them to find resources that are more comprehensive and fulfill the needs of the educational community. In other words, school librarians are effective in stretching school funds to meet the global needs of the school. A school library district supervisor was able to gain a pricing advantage on a database for the schools because the public library also purchased rights to the database. In addition, the school library supervisor continued to work with vendors to obtain resources the district needed. This particular school district served learners representing more than one hundred nationalities and speaking ninety-three different languages. As part of a deal with the database company, the school library supervisor negotiated inclusion of a language package so that parents could read information in a language they knew, thus empowering them to be involved with their learners' assignments. Each time school librarians provide economic answers by working with partners inside and outside the school, the school library as well as stakeholders benefit.

## Building on Accomplishments

When stakeholders in a school work together for a common goal, the partnerships that form create ready-made teams for future work. A principal in a secondary school felt excellence should be recognized. As a result, his school applied for the National Blue Ribbon Schools Program. It was an enormous undertaking for the staff. And, yes, the school librarian was asked to chair the committee to pull the documentation together. She broke down the application process into five different steps and asked fellow educators to chair the step that matched their skills strength. As a result of partnering with all stakeholders from the school community, the school received the National Blue Ribbon Schools designation. Building on the accomplishment of applying for the National Blue Ribbon Schools Program, the school librarian then applied for AASL's National School Library of the Year Award. The process was a lot of work, but the school staff once again teamed up to successfully achieve the National School Library of the Year Award. Two important results for the school library came from the AASL award. First, the school librarian was validated multiple times by stakeholders who came to support the school library as a necessary and essential part of learners' educational experiences. Second, because of the award, the school principal consistently and openly praised the work of the school librarian and the library program.

# Roles Foster Relationships

School librarians have access to several levels of relationships through the inter-connected roles they perform each day. Through their roles as leaders, instructional partners, information specialists, teachers, and program administrators, school librarians launch meaningful partnerships. These roles, represented in figure I.1, are a natural entry into building successful partnerships for the school library. The participation of each of these stakeholders increases the school librarian's ability to accomplish goals and achieve key strategic directions for the school library. In their daily activities, school librarians practice and develop their negotiating, alli-ance-building, and collaboration skills, which are essential to shaping partnerships. Partnerships become a natural outcome when connections are successfully made with learners, educators, administrators, and parents.

## *Leader*

"Leadership and librarianship go hand in hand. So many of the skills and disposi-tions needed to be an effective leader are the very same skills librarians employ to ensure their students are successful" (Martin 2013, 175). Leaders create partnerships as a method of accomplishing important goals. A step toward the achievement of a school library goal is to create a common objective with stakeholders that satisfies a shared goal. Using the concept of building partnerships to achieve shared goals requires learning the art of compromise. Jayson DeMers (2017), founder and CEO of AudienceBloom, enumerated the basics for achieving positive compromises. The most important part of the strategy is to listen to the other person and find common ground for agreement. This is a starting point for attaining buy-in because by listen-ing to what is important to other educators, the school librarian gains insight about specific elements of the school library vision and objectives that will be supported. After agreement has been reached on a joint objective, the identification of mutual expectations provides clarity that prompts creation of an action plan. For example, when a new district library supervisor inherited an office staff of eight employees who had been working in isolation rather than as a team, the supervisor brought each staff member in for a conversation that included asking what was important to that person. The supervisor also asked each employee to explain the purpose of the department for the school libraries in the district. This discussion was the beginning of finding common ground to attain buy-in for forming a strong central office team. At the first monthly staff meeting, the employees developed a set of common goals for the department. These goals unified all central office staff members' efforts toward the goal of becoming essential to the school librarians in the field. As part of an action plan, the supervisor required all support staff members to visit an elementary and a secondary school library and report what they observed. The support staff also were charged with asking the school librarians what was most helpful from the central office staff and what other services would help them in their school libraries. The outcomes of these visits were shared at monthly meetings, and a motivated central office team evolved. The cataloging staff, acquisitions staff, bookkeeper, secretary, and technology staff began to experience a shared vision. More important, they found ways to help each other and streamline the processes they performed, which resulted in quicker response times for the school libraries.

Another part of relationship building is knowing how to effectively manage time. School librarians as leaders must acknowledge their time limitations as well as those of educators working with them. To achieve solid support, the school librarian needs to assess how much time to devote to attaining a compromise versus determining at what point to delay the project for a future time. Essential to this decision is thinking through what the outcome will be if the partnership *does not* form. The aim is not just to attain a goal but to build positive energy through collaboration. Hoping to build partnerships, the school librarian shows leadership by offering alternative ideas for implementation that may make the project more useful for both the school library and the partnering department. It is at this stage that the school librarian needs to draw a mental line between what is absolutely nonnegotiable and what is not necessarily essential. In other words, how important is this issue, goal, or idea? At this point the school librarian needs to keep the negotiating positive so that a resolution and a plan result and the partnership can proceed forward. DeMers (2017) reminded readers to remain professional throughout the interaction, which will set the stage for future collaborative partnerships. Following these guidelines develops the negotiation and collaboration skills needed to form partnerships.

### Instructional Partner

The school librarian collaborates with other educators to develop learning experiences that integrate AASL's learner Domains and Competencies with curriculum content. As instructional connections between school librarians and educators expand and diversify, the bases for meaningful partnerships increase. The role of instructional partner provides the school librarian with insight into the curriculum needs of educators, which increases the school librarian's awareness of resource needs. Working with educators assists the school librarian with customizing resources and instruction for diverse learners. School librarians have the advantage of knowing learners over the span of their time at the school. As a result, school librarians are able to provide in-depth insight to educators about individual learners. Working one-on-one with educators on curriculum design opens pathways for the school librarian to transform the educators' passions into unique programs and learning experiences. The opportunities that arise from the instructional partner role during each collaborative project provide important relationship-building opportunities.

## Information Specialist

With the continued availability of technology tools, the school librarian is in a position to create global learning experiences in which understanding of varied cultures is possible. School librarians are charged to showcase "learners' reflections on their place within the global learning community" (AASL 2018a, School Librarian II.D.3.). This interaction with learners develops connections through which school librarians can invite learners' participation in and contributions to library projects and plans. The educators who work with these same learners create collaborative projects with school librarians that are grounded in the ethical use of information. This interchange provides an opportunity for the school librarian, educators, and learners to model safe, responsible, ethical, and legal information behaviors in lesson development and in their personal relations (AASL 2018a, School Librarian VI.D.3.).

## Teacher

As teacher, the school librarian creates "an atmosphere in which learners feel empowered and interactions are learner-initiated" (AASL 2018a, School Librarian II.D.1.). Developing these competencies in learners provides school librarians opportunities to construct practices that strengthen their own empowerment and lead to stakeholder interactions. Many of the Competencies in the Shared Foundations encourage school librarians to teach learners to be inclusive. As school librarians generate activities and projects that foster understanding of different cultures, they are also creating acceptance for the diversity found in their library and school. Empowerment and inclusivity produce an environment that supports partnership building. Daily, school librarians in their teacher role reinforce practices that nurture and build partnerships with educators and learners.

## Program Administrator

Further partnerships with the educational community result when school librarians serve as program administrators. "The implementation of a successful school library program requires the collaborative development of the program mission, strategic plan, and policies, as well as the effective management of staff, the program budget, and the physical and virtual spaces" (AASL 2018a, 15). Each of these tasks involves working with representatives of the school community by creating committees and task forces. The key to forming an effective committee is to select members who are diverse thinkers and who can contribute positively to the work needing to be accomplished. In trying to ensure that all voices are represented, sometimes committees are too large. Keeping the number of committee members to five or six permits active participation. As program administrator, the school librarian should be organized and prepared for meetings with an agenda, data, and accompanying resources. The school librarian needs to set a time for the meeting that considers when members are available, especially those who represent administrators, parents, and community members. The partnerships resulting from collaborative committees and task forces form an advocacy team as new library policies and procedures bring change to the library.

## Increasing Effective Partnerships

Forming alliances and partnerships to generate support for school library initiatives creates more lasting change, partly because when school librarians and stakeholders contribute to transforming the educational environment by working together, their participation creates ownership in the results. A lasting partnership is the outcome of specific intentional actions that increase trust between the school librarian and the educational community's stakeholders. One way that school librarians build trust is to "work effectively with others to broaden perspectives and work toward common goals" (AASL 2018a, 85). Working effectively involves finding out who is dependable, motivated, and responsible. Each of these dispositions demonstrated consistently over time develops a reciprocal trust between stakeholders. School librarians who have a reputation for getting things done know who makes a difference for projects. They work jointly with educators, learners, and other stakeholders who support the ideas that define a project. School librarians who encourage active participation in the school library goals use problem-solving and critical-thinking competencies to elicit direct input from educators, learners, and parents. These partnerships form as a result of shared goals. In addition, partnerships develop because the school library supports active participation by "creating and maintaining a learning environment that supports and stimulates discussion from all members of the school community" (AASL 2018a, School Library III.D.1.). Trust, active participation, shared responsibility, and mutual objectives are internalized to form long-lasting successful partnerships.

## Managing Multiple Partnerships

As partnerships develop over time, school librarians must learn to manage the growing number of relationships to maintain successful results. Not only do school librarians have internal and external stakeholders, they also have professional organizations and their state department of education with which to partner. Prioritizing is extremely important in maintaining a focus on school library goals and keeping projects moving forward. One way to manage multiple relationships is to create a visual of current commitments by generating time lines for projects and then placing them in a calendar. Time lines provide a plan for working with multiple groups. Time lines also provide a balance that keeps projects current and moving. School librarians need to be flexible and adjust schedules on the fly. Organizing each day to provide time and energy to nurture stakeholder groups is valuable for maintaining partnerships. School librarians also need to be open to recruiting a partner to deal with a facet of the project that is missing coverage. Being aware of the expertise that local, state, and national professional organizations provide for school library projects may save valuable time by contributing connections to helpful resources. School librarians who invest their skills and expertise in professional organizations and their state department of education find that those partnerships enable them to remain in the forefront of the profession.

## Connecting to the Shared Foundations

For school librarians, there are various reasons for forming partnerships with stakeholders. These partnerships reap internal benefits for the school library, such as strong instructional collaborative lessons with other educators, and external benefits, such as gaining the support of an outside community organization that will supply resources for the school library. Using AASL and its resources as the national school library organization provides a foundation of authority for creating partnerships and strengthening the results of those partnerships. Focusing on the developmental Domain of Grow in the School Librarian and School Library Frameworks within the Shared Foundations of Include, Collaborate, and Engage maximizes school librarians' ability to create partnerships and further develop the five school librarian roles in their practice.

---

 ### INCLUDE

School librarians serve as leaders and teachers when they "explicitly lead learners to demonstrate empathy and equity in knowledge building within the global learning community by initiating opportunities that allow learners to demonstrate interest in other perspectives" (AASL 2018a, School Librarian II.D.2.). School librarians meet this Competency by sharing the process or products facilitated in the school library through social media, apps, websites, or blogs. Another way school librarians meet this Competency is by reaching out to the global community for expert information that in turn becomes a resource for research being done in the classroom or school library. This opportunity to look outward to the global learning community for expert information that offers other perspectives broadens everyone's mindset and leads to richer conversations and information sharing. Classroom educators rely on school librarians' expertise to fulfill the role of instructional partner in looking outward for optimal resources. This partnership is strengthened and the relationship is built when the school librarian takes the initiative and creates opportunities to form deeper knowledge bases.

"Clearly and frequently articulating the school library's impact when communicating with administration, faculty, staff, learners, parents, and the community" is one of the most important and yet can be one of the hardest jobs of the school librarian as program administrator (AASL 2018a, School Library II.D.3.). Finding the right time and choosing the best delivery method are crucial for ensuring optimum impact on the stakeholders. Showing how different demographic groups' needs are being met by the school library is an important component of the articulation of impact. Examples of the school library's impact include instructional and reading activities designed and implemented, collection development decisions made, and monetary resources being spent on different materials, all to benefit the larger school community. The articulation can be done using words, images, or both, depending on the audience. Images and words can be used in posts on social media and digital storytelling through apps to reach the outside community. Statistics and images are best used in infographics to share impact data with building-level and district administrators. Words, when spoken by the learners and classroom educators themselves, can serve as strong tools to communicate the impact of the school library to the larger stakeholder community. This stakeholder community ranges from the immediate building level to the larger AASL community. Being conscientious in formulating how the impact is articulated will stimulate forming partnerships and building relationships at all community levels.

## COLLABORATE

School librarians foster active participation, learning is a social responsibility, and information is a shared resource (AASL 2018a, School Librarian III.D.2., School Library III.D.2.). These are all powerful statements emphasized in the Grow Domain of the Collaborate Shared Foundation in the School Librarian and School Library Frameworks, and ones that school librarians embrace with their decisions in the school library. School librarians realize that active participation in learning is not limited to young learners but includes fellow educators and district-level colleagues. For example, school librarians who consistently formulate and present professional development for building- or district-level colleagues help them access and interact with the newest resources available through the school library. The professional development could highlight the availability of district databases, AASL resources, or information technologies, all to benefit instruction and the larger school community's needs.

The ideals that learning is a social responsibility and that information is a shared resource become the guiding forces and implicit expectations for stakeholders to become invested in and benefit from the school library. "Collaborative efforts create more-holistic results than individual efforts alone" (AASL 2018a, 87). These ideals are implemented in well-designed instructional plans, physical space allocation for different functions, and virtual activities that encourage collaboration. School librarians at every level can initiate the opportunity for partnerships with educators, learners, and parents by offering learners time to give presentations on topics of interest in the school library. A high school library was successful when it partnered with the business department to facilitate a runway show to be given in the school library, preparing students for prom season. Connections were made with the community for resources to support the event, and assessments were given to the students on their decisions leading to the event. A middle school library received strong community support when learners' makerspace creations that solved environmental issues were posted on the school's website. More people were exposed to the creation process and products by sharing them digitally with the larger community. An elementary school library's space was used as the information and welcome center for a school-wide PTA literacy event, reinforcing to the parents the integral role of the school library as the hub of the school. When stakeholders, with the school librarian's lead, embody the ideals and see evidence of learning as a social responsibility and information as a shared resource, then the school library's potential as an agent of change and promoter of partnerships is realized.

## ENGAGE

The Grow Domain in the Engage Shared Foundation for the School Librarian and School Library Frameworks focuses on decisions that affect the learning environment of the school library. "School librarians support learners' engagement with information to extend personal learning by structuring a learning environment for innovative use of information and information technologies" (AASL 2018a, School Librarian VI.D.1.). What does it look like to be innovative in information use? How can information technologies support learners' engagement with information? How does forming partnerships with other educators facilitate innovation in the school library? These are questions that need to be considered before school librarians can meet this Competency. Taking the initiative to reach out to technology educators or administrators at the building and district levels to offer their expertise is an important step in structuring a learning environment that fosters innovation. This expertise can range from introducing new information technologies to integrating the technologies into the school library during a building-level or district-wide meeting. As instructional partner, the school librarian works to form positive partnerships to build a stimulating learning environment, thereby extending the impact of the school library to all stakeholders.

The role of program administrator of the school library is multifaceted and is often unseen by stakeholders. It requires making well-informed decisions in order to be effective. "The school library supports individual responsibility for information use by providing an environment in which the school librarian can effectively develop, direct, and promote resources, services, policies, procedures, and programming aligned with current standards, ethical codes, and principles of the education and information professions" (AASL 2018a, School Library VI.D.1.). School librarians need the backing of administration, at the building and district levels, to provide the appropriate environment and encourage partnerships within the school. Maintaining this key partnership with administration is crucial to the overall success of the school library. The positive results of the partnership can be seen when parental concerns arise, when school leadership teams include school librarians, and when the school library is able to meet school-wide needs. For example, a principal, a school librarian, and classroom educators designed a checkout schedule in which upper elementary classes would visit the school library once a month. This schedule ensured that all learners and educators had consistent and dedicated time to access the school library resources and pleasure reading materials.

Forming partnerships with the surrounding larger community makes the school library environment strong as well. Successful partnerships can result in receiving grant money from district educational foundations, reading materials from retail stores, and makerspace materials from companies. School librarians need to be intentional in making time to show the larger community, through actions and words, how the community's contributions positively impact learning in the school library. This appreciation reinforces the relationships and helps the school library form other possible partnerships.

## Promoting Partnerships

Partnerships with stakeholders are beneficial in helping school librarians realize the scope of the school library's impact. Strategies for promoting partnerships include maximizing the five roles of the school librarian, utilizing the expertise of the stakeholders, and providing resources to meet the global needs of the community. Incorporating the Grow Domain within the Shared Foundations of Include, Collaborate, and Engage from the School Librarian and School Library Frameworks serves as a foundation for making decisions that facilitate the success of the partnerships. The results of the decisions range from the quality of the resources available through partnerships to opportunities for active participation to enrich the experience of the school library. The idea that "learning is a social responsibility" is compelling and leads school librarians to take the initiative to form authentic partnerships with stakeholders (AASL, School Librarian III.D.2.). Promoting partnerships is improved by focusing on the "developmental" Domain of Grow (AASL 2018a, 15) in the School Librarian and School Library Frameworks within the Shared Foundations of Include, Collaborate, and Engage and maximizes school librarians' ability to create partnerships and further develop the five school librarian roles in their practice.

# 11

# Self-Awareness

Self-awareness is essential to personal growth, enabling school librarians to focus on their strengths. "Research shows that people are much more engaged [and have a greater sense of well-being] when they work within their strengths" ("Strengths" 2017). Beginning with the publication of *Information Power,* AASL's learning standards focused on life skills that learners need to be successful. Critical-thinking, problem-solving, and developing dispositions evoked deeper growth for learners by providing understanding and meaning to their work as learners. Likewise, school librarians use these same dispositions to self-examine their own motivations. The result is that school librarians benefit from self-awareness by understanding the set of values that influences their work. Integrating these beliefs into the five roles of leader, instructional partner, information specialist, teacher, and program administrator provides opportunities for school librarians to intentionally serve as change agents to make the school library and instructional environment more dynamic.

## LIFE SKILLS THAT MATTER

Self-Awareness: "The ability to take an honest look at your life without attachment to it being right or wrong."

—Debbie Ford
Source: https://lifeskillsthatmatter.com/self-awareness

## Assessing Self-Awareness

"Lifelong learning, a process of continuous improvement, permeates every aspect of an effective school library" (AASL 2018a, 148). Through self-awareness of strengths and weaknesses, the school librarian is consistently exploring opportunities for personal and professional growth. The confidence that results from personal self-assessment is critical to the program administrator role of the school librarian. An assessment strategy for developing self-awareness begins with recognizing values, beliefs, and dispositions in others. The idea behind recognizing abilities and assets in others is that it exposes evidence of those specific characteristics in the observer. When AASL first introduced dispositions to school librarians, there was confusion about how to instruct learners on an intangible such as persistence. Teaching learners dispositions caused concern. A secondary school librarian in the role of teacher decided to identify, measure, and strengthen her own dispositions by observing learners' actions in the library. Daily, the school librarian focused on identifying a different disposition. When a learner displayed that attribute, the school librarian made a note detailing the action and the context in which the disposition was observed. Next, the school librarian handwrote a postcard to the learner's guardians acknowledging the positive results from the learner's actions. For example, on one postcard, the school librarian explained that she was impressed with "Joe" when he demonstrated motivation by seeking information to answer a research question and then went beyond the academic requirements of the project by identifying misconceptions and conflicting information in order to gain a broader perspective of the topic. Over time this school librarian became adept at recognizing dispositions in learners and recognizing the very same dispositions in herself. This self-awareness provided the school librarian with insight into her strengths as well as areas that needed to be improved. Self-awareness helped her to understand the intention behind her actions, decisions, and motivations.

## Benefits of Self-Awareness

Self-awareness is crucial for successful relationships within the school. It reveals the motivation behind program initiatives mandated by educators and administrators. School librarians who thoughtfully evaluate each interaction they make to determine what went well, what did not go well, and what they would do differently next time gain insight into relationships within the school. Self-aware school librarians know why they do the things that they do. Their introspection helps them learn from mistakes and provides them with ways to improve relationships that benefit the school library.

As program administrators, school librarians recognize their library stakeholders' needs. Educators and learners require support from the school librarian for academic and literacy skills. The process of determining why and how personal values impact the selection of library materials is helpful when school librarians choose resources. For example, schools with diverse learners need materials that are leveled and varied. Reading reviews and seeking input from educators of learners with unique needs are responsibilities of the school librarian when selecting resources. By exploring and understanding the values that influence collection decisions, the self-aware school librarian creates a strong library that is based on stakeholder needs.

Another benefit of self-awareness is evident when intellectual freedom issues arise. "School librarians are responsible for fostering one of America's most cherished freedoms: the freedom of speech and freedom to hear what others have to say" (AASL 2018a, 13). Providing learners with choices is important for a balanced collection. Sometimes conflicts arise between parent values and content in library resources, conflicts that challenge school librarians' professional responsibility. In situations like this it is important to remove personal emotions by referring to collection development policies. When questions from parents arise, a strong materials review process ensures that school librarians meet the needs of learners and educators while addressing parental concerns. A self-aware school librarian removes any personal reasons for defending a material and lets the complaint work through the process. Ensuring that intellectual freedom is every learners' and educators' right is the job responsibility of the school librarian.

When school librarians are aware of their strengths, they are then able to intentionally use these assets to deepen their professionalism. For example, self-awareness provides immediate knowledge of who upsets you, is a barometer of when you need help, and helps to set up boundaries to reduce stress. In each of these situations, the school librarian who reflects on the root cause of daily encounters can compensate by preplanning how to manage people, find additional sources of manpower, and control the everyday hassles that create distress. Digging deep to own the professional values and beliefs that govern actions and reactions increases school librarians' professionalism.

## Building Confidence

Self-awareness is critical to developing the confidence necessary to meet challenges in an environment where competing needs and interests create tension and conflict. Limited funding in the education community creates anxiety as departments in the school vie for fixed materials and people resources. These opposing forces demand that school librarians, serving in the role of program administrator, develop confidence to confront any barriers that emerge preventing school library success.

A district library supervisor was silent at meetings with the decision makers because she lacked confidence. As leader of the district library program, she needed to be confident in her presentation of information. Instead, as each new idea by curriculum directors impacted the school library, she was meek and honest in her knowledge of school library best practices. When other curriculum supervisors protected their areas in meetings, her voice was lost as more vocal educators bartered for their programs. Her lack of self-confidence hampered her ability to effectively convince others of key elements critical to the school library program. Perhaps more distressful was that this district supervisor lacked awareness of why the school library program was in a downward spiral. Her lack of awareness of her own part in the loss of school library support prevented her from fixing the situation.

Building confidence begins with reflection. Self-reflection is a fundamental aspect of evaluation and is a critical component of the Domain Grow. This Domain includes the school librarian's ability to recognize and acknowledge that a growth mindset is needed for professional improvement. This growth mindset can be developed, improved, and expanded when a school librarian maintains an open attitude toward continuous improvement. An effective method for improving the disposition of confidence is to review what occurred during a meeting with an administrator or with educators. Thinking back over what was said, the reactions of those in the meeting, and evidence of how decisions were made provides concrete information on how to improve interactions to achieve success in the future. It is important to know details from the meeting to interpret the meaning behind decision makers' and educators' reactions. The school librarian who serves as leader and program administrator will then form a plan that guarantees that arguments and processes for introducing key points will be replicated to achieve success in future meetings.

Affirming thoughts can make a difference when developing confidence. A school librarian was receiving intimidating messages from her principal. The messages were causing her to question her value, and she responded by avoiding any interaction with the principal. Once she reflected on the situation, she decided to stay positive and took on the mantra of Eleanor Roosevelt: "No one can make you feel inferior without your consent."[1] And the school librarian maintained a positive outlook by responding professionally to the principal. Over time the principal softened and openly acknowledged the expertise of the school librarian, thus validating her role as a leader and instructional partner in the school.

## Making Decisions

Self-understanding guides school librarians to recognize the rationale and personal motives behind the decisions they make. Self-understanding provides a path to removing emotionalism and preconceived beliefs before making decisions. Reflecting on recent decisions, school librarians can analyze what beliefs and values influence their thinking. It may be helpful to list factors that influence opinions by evaluating how these views impact library instruction, policies, and procedures. The result is decisions that are professional and based on facts.

A district library supervisor resolved to find out what each school board member valued and supported. One board member wanted learners with limited English to succeed and supported programs that helped these learners achieve academically. The library supervisor created a committee composed of school librarians and other educators who worked with learners with limited English. The committee's charge was to research instructional best practices to use with learners with limited English. The committee also was asked to compile a list of resources needed by English learners and educators to encourage the development of literacy. The list of resources was then sent to a vendor who created a price quote. The district library supervisor presented the results of the committee's work to the district committee that worked on English learner policies and programs. Sitting on the district committee was the school board member who was a champion for learners with limited English. As a result of the presentation, the school board member urged the school board to fund the purchase of the resources for each of the schools with English learners. The decision by the school library supervisor to create an English learner committee had a positive outcome for the school libraries. An added outcome of the English learner initiative was the positive professional relationship that developed between the district library supervisor and the school board member.

As program administrators, school librarians make professional decisions that reflect core values and are based on self-awareness. Through self-awareness school librarians know that their values are supported and guided by the AASL Common Beliefs to ensure equitable learning opportunities for learners.

## Connecting to the Shared Foundations

Awareness of yourself as the school librarian and awareness of the school library's role in the overall school community are important mindsets to develop and practice in order to maximize the potential of the school library. These mindsets are pertinent to each other because decisions made by school librarians impact the entire school library. These mindsets include wanting to have stakeholders involved in the school library, modeling and striving for effective self-reflection, and staying educated about district and educational initiatives that affect the school library. To develop these mindsets, school librarians must be willing to be leaders in situations, ask clarifying questions of themselves and others, and look at the larger school community as a whole. The Grow Domain for Include, Collaborate, and Engage in the School Librarian and School Library Frameworks best embodies the development of these mindsets. "Looking at the dimensions of professional activity through the lens of the Shared Foundations (Inquire, Include, Collaborate, Curate, Explore, and Engage) provides school librarians with a framework for reflection and self-assessment to achieve personal professional growth that supports empowerment of learners and of the school librarian" (AASL 2018a, 148).

## INCLUDE

The Key Commitment for the Shared Foundation Include is to "demonstrate an understanding of and commitment to inclusiveness and respect for diversity in the learning community" (AASL 2018a, 76). Making this powerful one-word Shared Foundation, Include, and its Key Commitment a reality requires school librarians to know how best to build relationships with stakeholders in order for everyone to become more self-aware about their own impact on the success of the school library. "School librarians explicitly lead learners to demonstrate empathy and equity in knowledge building within the global learning community by showcasing learners' reflections on their place within the global learning community" (AASL 2018a, School Librarian II.D.3.). To meet this Competency, the school librarian needs to ask out loud important questions such as these: What does showcasing look like? Who does it reach? How can I stimulate learners to realize their part in, and to want to share their reflections with, the larger global community? What kind of self-assessment tool best facilitates articulation of the learners' reflections? When these questions are discussed by the school librarian and learners together, the answers are stronger, and the communication becomes more authentic.

"The school library builds empathy and equity within the global learning community by enabling equitable access to learning opportunities, academic and social support, and other resources necessary for learners' success" (AASL 2018a, School Library II.D.2.). This Alignment empowers the school librarian to realize the need to be self-aware enough to decide what resources are needed for academic and social support. It is the school librarian's responsibility to provide equitable access so all stakeholders, including parents, feel a part of the global learning community. The determination of resource needs and subgroup needs is made after reading data, asking clarifying questions, and initiating conversations with stakeholders. This inclusion promotes empathy and equity between the subgroups of the larger community. This Alignment can be seen in action when school librarians are active members of the school leadership team and are part of the conversations on demographic and academic strengths and weaknesses. Because school librarians service all members of the school, they are able to realize which resources are utilized by different people for academic and social support. Bringing this big picture perspective to the leadership team when making decisions about school goals and learners' growth gives school librarians the opportunity to share their expertise as information specialists and instructional partners as well as their investment in meeting the goals.

## COLLABORATE

The Grow Domain of the Shared Foundation Collaborate in the School Librarian and School Library Frameworks focuses on "active learner participation" (AASL 2018a). In order for the Competencies and Alignments to be met, self-aware school librarians understand that learners can be different people depending on the situation in the school library. This self-awareness allows school librarians to intentionally get stakeholders involved and active and helps to build relationships both within and outside the school library.

To foster active participation in learning situations, school librarians stimulate "learners to actively contribute to group discussions" with the understanding that "learning is a social responsibility" (AASL 2018a, School Librarian III.D.1., III.D.2.). Through their actions and words, school librarians help inspire learners to realize that contributing to their own learning in the school library makes the experience richer and more authentic. This aspect can be seen in a professional development session in which the classroom educators share ideas about how best to utilize the resources for upcoming units. This can be seen when learners write or visualize how they process a topic they chose to study. This can be seen when administrators, at the building and district levels, discuss a school library's statistics—number of circulated items, number of classes taught, number of learners and educators reached—and realize the impact on the larger school community. This can be seen when parents attend a literacy night and discover new school library resources available to enrich learning at home.

"Creating and maintaining a learning environment that supports and stimulates discussion from all members of the school community" is an important component of a successful school library (AASL 2018a, School Library III.D.1.). This Alignment can be met when the school librarian takes time to ask genuine clarifying questions of all members of the school community, with the intention of using the answers to expand the services of the school library. Indira Gandhi reinforced this approach when she said, "The power to question is the basis of all human progress."[2] The questions and answers can happen through informal conversations, a consistent online form on the website about a particular topic, intermittent surveys throughout the year to gather data, or questions and data that are posted in the school library. The types of clarifying questions can range from asking learners about book choices to asking administrators about scheduling decisions to asking parents about accessing resources to asking educators about upcoming classroom topics. When stakeholders realize that the school librarian is genuinely interested in their opinions and thoughts, the learning environment becomes more welcoming and inclusive for everyone, thus building stronger relationships with the stakeholders.

## ENGAGE

"Championing and modeling safe, responsible, ethical, and legal information behaviors" is one of the most crucial responsibilities of the school librarian (AASL 2018a, School Librarian VI.D.3.). "As part of the school library's dedication to ethical behavior, the school librarian also models and promotes the highest standards of conduct, ethics, and integrity in the use of all types of resources" (AASL 2018a, 117). The importance of this modeling for all stakeholders cannot be overstated. School librarians need to be self-aware enough to know whether they are championing and modeling behaviors sincerely. Whether championing and modeling behaviors occurs through an instructional lesson plan, a faculty professional development session, or a school-sponsored family event, the effect is the same. The stakeholders realize that the school librarian is a reliable resource for learners and the larger school community to utilize. This belief in the reliability of the school librarian will raise the level of service cultivated by the school library. Modeling best practice when engaging with print and digital resources fulfills the roles of teacher, information specialist, and program administrator.

Being self-aware as a school librarian also includes taking the initiative to stay informed about current education and information technology professional trends for the purpose of making decisions about the school library. "The school library supports individual responsibility for information use by providing an environment in which the school librarian can effectively develop, direct, and promote resources, services, policies, procedures, and programming aligned with current standards, ethical codes, and principles of the education and information professions" (AASL 2018a, School Library VI.D.1.). As program administrator, the school librarian is responsible for learning about district- and building-level initiatives that impact the learning community. The next step is to identify how the school library can choose resources to help implement the initiatives. For example, a district created a learner profile during an academic school year as a structured vision to guide instruction and provide a framework for decisions being made in the county. The learner profile included attributes and skills that students need in order to be best prepared for life and a deeper learning model for how to integrate the skills into action (HCPS 2018b). The central office library services district leadership provided guidance to immediately make connections with the AASL Standards Integrated Frameworks and created a graphic to show the connections (figure 11.1). Building-level school librarians were taught, through well-thought-out professional development, how best to implement the learner profile in instructional lessons, STEAM and literacy-based activities, and collection development decisions. Both building-level and district administrators are now able to see daily how the school libraries promote the learner profile for all stakeholders.

School librarians are leaders when they take time to practice self-awareness in order to develop their professional skills and create stronger relationships with stakeholders. This self-awareness leads to more effective clarifying questions in conversations and lessons, better interactive professional development sessions for educators, and stronger resource decisions based on data. All these results lead to increased participation by stakeholders in the school library, benefiting the larger school community.

**FIGURE 11.1**

## Henrico learner profile aligned to AASL Standards

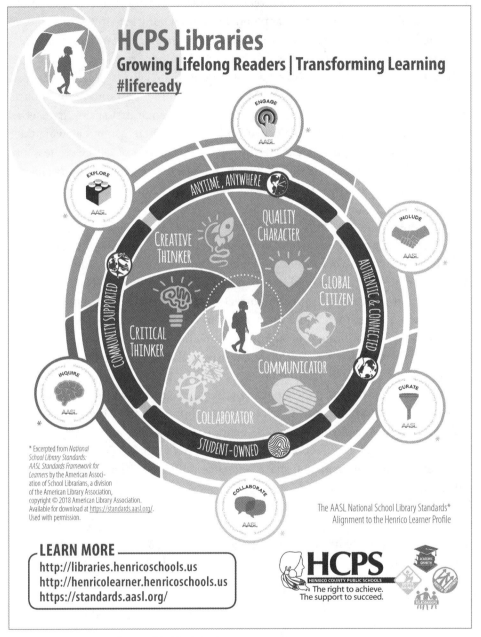

Source: Henrico County (Virginia) Public Schools

## Impacts of Self-Awareness

Being present in the moment is a direct result of school librarians' achievement of self-awareness. Their introspection benefits school librarians in the five roles of leader, instructional partner, information specialist, teacher, and program administrator. Understanding why decisions are made and actions are taken is an outcome of the internal clarity that follows reflection and ultimately leads to self-awareness. School librarians who know why and how the environment around them impacts their thoughts have a greater opportunity to achieve the goals they set for themselves and for the school library. The reflective work they complete when reviewing their daily actions and decisions transforms the intangible concept of self-awareness into tangible indicators of success or failure and the reasons for these outcomes. From this self-examination, a plan is developed to ensure that future decisions and actions are productive.

Self-awareness is critical to understanding the meaning behind relationships. In each of the five roles that school librarians perform, relationship building takes school libraries to a higher level of acceptance and performance. This outcome is due to strengthening the school librarian's show of confidence, which stimulates optimism and risk taking. Optimism attracts stakeholders to the school librarian and encourages them to embrace change that may otherwise seem risky.

The goal of school librarians is growth. Growth of leadership skills developed through self-awareness. Growth in relationships that work together for equity, global learning, active participation by stakeholders, and responsible use of information. To instill a culture of academic and personal growth for the learning community, school librarians need to experience and practice the Competencies and Alignments from the Grow Domain of Include, Collaborate, and Engage. School librarians who apply the School Librarian and School Library Frameworks to the improvement of relationships foster a reflective philosophy that leads to positive self-awareness.

### NOTES

1. https://www.brainyquote.com/quotes/eleanor_roosevelt_161321
2. https://www.brainyquote.com/quotes/indira_gandhi_163281

# Empowerment

# 12

There is a hotel in New York City called **Library Hotel. At this hotel** there are ten guest room floors, and each one pays tribute to a specific Dewey Decimal Classification category. To carry the theme further, each room has a collection of art and books related to one distinct topic within the Dewey Decimal category assigned to the floor. This uniquely themed hotel routinely receives the highest rating available in reviews. Customers attest to the attentive and cordial staff, who are cited as helpful and knowledgeable. After their stay in the hotel, some guests were amazed by the customer service provided, stating that the location and amenities were great but that the staff took it over the top ("A Book Lover's Paradise" 2018). Receiving accolades is often the result of employee empowerment when employees are given the freedom, flexibility, and power to make decisions and solve problems (Saylor Foundation 2013). Businesses understand the importance of empowerment to overall performance and quality of work. School librarians, as leaders and program administrators, benefit by incorporating empowerment strategies into the supervision and management of the school library.

## Empowering Stakeholders

School librarians who feel more secure making all the decisions will have difficulty implementing empowerment because the outcome of empowering others is developing stakeholders who thrive on shared responsibility. At the Library Hotel the workforce is trained to meet customer demands. Training is a key element when developing empowerment in individuals. Without individual empowerment every small decision becomes the responsibility of the school librarian, who is overloaded with many tasks and services to manage. For this reason, the school librarian encourages transformational leadership for educators, learners, and the community. Part of changing the school library culture is providing stakeholders with the skills to be confident decision makers and self-motivated individuals. Transforming the school library from a follower culture to an empowering culture can be accomplished through coaching, mentoring, and delegating.

## Coaching

It is difficult to think of coaching without reflecting on some of the amazing athletic coaches who set a standard that attracts players and fans to their team. Every day, the Duke University basketball team signs top recruits who want to train under Mike Krzyzewski. In addition, many assistant coaches know that working under the leadership of Mike Krzyzewski will develop their own skills. "As a coach, Krzyzewski's goal and strength has been to instill motivation—for each individual and for the team—to have every individual in a positive state of mind, utilizing abilities to their fullest, and not afraid to fail" (Coach K 2018). School librarians and district-level library supervisors who coach empowerment and leadership become incredibly successful because the individuals in their organization use their abilities to their fullest and are not afraid to fail—or succeed.

Coaching, like teaching, requires thoughtful planning that incorporates activities and decisions to build confidence and trust. Learners, educators, and community members must have trust in the school librarian to accept assignments and positions on committees. Trust is built over time and is the direct result of developing self-awareness and forming partnerships. Confidence develops when the actions taken to implement school library objectives are successful. The school librarian must base the rationale behind decisions on solid values. This approach provides the school librarian with a firm foundation on which confidence can grow. When a school librarian demonstrates confidence, this disposition will be assimilated by stakeholders.

Coaching is also preparing stakeholders for teamwork by modeling practices for teams to work effectively. For example, meetings are organized with agendas. As topics are discussed in committees, all team members are provided an opportunity to contribute to the conversation. In a well-run meeting, participants are provided opportunities to volunteer for assignments. These assignments may be research-based, or the school librarian may provide corroborated information related to the task for the team member to analyze. The school librarian needs to set completion dates for assignments. Finally, meetings should always end with a recap of what was accomplished and a breakdown of assignments for the committee members. "A coach and a leader measures actions, results, and efficiency. The information gathered when these measures are applied helps leaders create plans to achieve future goals" (Martin 2013, 46).

Part of coaching is the willingness to take risks. Pushing beyond uncertainty needs coaching from the school librarian. A risk-taking starting point is for school librarians to assume calculated risks. As research-oriented and data-driven individuals, school librarians collect information before making a risky decision or undertaking a precarious action. For example, a secondary school librarian decided to organize a One School, One Book project for the last five weeks of the school year. It seemed like a super idea because testing would be over and a community read would focus learners' energies in a positive direction. Before progressing with the idea, the school librarian contacted a colleague at the state library who had experience with large events like a community read. After the school librarian's discussion with the state librarian, it was obvious that creating a meaningful One School, One Book event would take months, not weeks, to accomplish. As a result, the school librarian put into motion a community read for the fall, with educators and learners reading the selected title over summer break. It was still a risky challenge to start, but with research the event was a calculated risk that in the end proved successful. Evaluation after the event exposed areas where improvements could be made. This literary experience continued for five years, spilling out into the greater metro area where businesses supported funding to bring the author to the area for an assembly with the district high school learners and another discussion for the larger community. This calculated risk empowered the school librarian to try more literacy efforts. Throughout the event, learners, educators, and community members were involved and coached through book talks, philanthropic events, and author preparations. Coaching allowed a program of this magnitude to take place because the work and responsibility were shared. The community became empowered through teamwork.

## *Mentoring*

Empowerment is enhanced in the school library both formally and informally. Formal mentoring is deliberate, and informal mentoring is impromptu. Every day the school librarian guides learners and educators by mentoring them. Perhaps the best mentoring comes when the school librarian uses both informal and formal mentoring. The strategies and goals for each are different, yet the outcome is relationship building that encourages a more self-reliant, confident, and knowledgeable individual. Ultimately an outcome of formal mentoring is continued friendship or informal mentoring.

Informal mentoring is the result of two individuals being accessible to each other. Because such mentoring is impromptu, often the goals are unspecified. The mentoring results from conversations and discussions that guide each individual through situations that emerge and need solving. Training is based on the mentor's experiences and knowledge. Advising is reciprocal, and both participants learn from each other. An elementary school librarian was new and felt a need for advice from someone who had experience in the district about routine library operations as well as guidance interpreting policies and procedures. When a question came up about book fair policy, the school librarian e-mailed another elementary school librarian in the district. From this beginning a strong collaborative relationship evolved as both school librarians informally mentored each other. Some professional organizations like AASL provide blogs and discussion lists whereby school librarians are informally mentored through the comments and insights of members. Informal mentoring in which friendships interconnect with personal learning is a strong tool for developing empowerment in school librarians.

Formal mentoring is more planned and structured. A school district's library department was known nationally for the mentoring program it developed. An elementary school librarian was enthusiastic about mentoring. She contacted the district library supervisor and, with the assistance of the district professional development office, designed a program entitled Collaborating Partnerships because both parties would benefit. The program is still strong and is a two-way mentoring process whereby the experienced school librarian is teamed with a "new to the district" school librarian. Incorporating a structured training plan into the program expands its effectiveness. For example, vendors of the library management system provide sessions on how to best use the software. Technology experts provide training on new software so that the school librarians are first in the school to model emerging technologies and teach their learners and educators. Intellectual freedom discussions explain the school board policy for reviewing instructional materials. Collaborating Partnerships was designed as a one-year program, but many school librarians wanted to continue as "experienced mentors" during their second year in the district. As they continue in the program, participants are empowered to share their experience with others.

## Delegating

One of the most valuable empowerment strategies is to effectively delegate tasks. Unfortunately, delegating is sometimes used not as an empowerment tool but as a way to do less. "Delegation is assigning responsibility for outcomes along with the authority to do what is needed to produce the desired results" (Lloyd, n.d.). Successful school librarians provide volunteers and clerical assistants increasing responsibility for tasks. Like walking a tightrope, there is tension between the task delegated and the skill level needed to accomplish the job. Crossing the wire too fast might disrupt the tension and result in failure, but taking small, incremental steps increases the potential for success.

Empowerment results when school librarians train their volunteers and clerical assistants to expand their skill sets. Understanding what competencies individuals possess provides the school librarian with a starting point. Taking time to create a plan for the volunteer or clerical assistant is important in the beginning. The plan should include a time line for completing the work and check-in points along the way. The check-in points provide insight about whether the individual is on the right track or whether assistance is needed. Empowerment results when the school librarian takes individuals to another level of responsibility and decision making with each completed task. The bottom line when delegating is to know your people and to recognize their individual skills. After providing parameters for completing a task, let go and let them do the job. *Trust* them!

## Multidimensional Empowerment

Empowerment is not linear but multidimensional and builds on self-awareness. Empowerment depends on school librarians' understanding of the motives and values behind their actions, which is self-awareness. Empowerment also requires analysis of the concrete actions that school librarians take as well as identification of processes that require improvement. School librarians need to examine the five interconnected roles they perform, depicted in figure I.1, and incorporate empowerment into each role. They do this by influencing and encouraging learners and educators to progress beyond their current goal and skill to the next level of performance. For learners this process includes academic empowerment, and for educators this process involves professional empowerment. Examining the five roles of leader, instructional partner, information specialist, teacher, and program administrator offers opportunities for the school librarian to empower learners and educators.

### *Leaders Empower*

"Leaders who empower others also seek to advance colleagues into leadership by sharing responsibility. Delegating the responsibility in progressive waves of accountability is essential to support colleagues' growth" (Martin 2013, 117–118). The school librarian as leader has opportunities to empower learners and educators. Learners are empowered when they are encouraged to reflect on their learning and then seek alternate solutions. Educators are empowered when the school librarian uses a committee structure and involves stakeholders in the decisions needed to make changes and improvements to the school library. Partnerships and self-awareness are essential for building stakeholder relationships and, in turn, form the building blocks of successful empowerment. Trust, listening, and a culture of lifelong learning are qualities that encourage empowerment among stakeholders. School librarians who are leaders develop these qualities through collaborating and openly seeking stakeholder input. When professional organizations pursue school librarians to serve as volunteer leaders, they do so by opening a connection through which both the organization and the school librarian benefit. Shared responsibility that is encouraged by the school librarian steadily advances mutual accountability and leads to empowerment.

## Instructional Partners Empower

As an instructional partner, the school librarian collaborates with other educators to create instructional experiences that engage learners. This partnership forms trust and confidence as educators and school librarians learn from each other. By sharing ideas and individual expertise, school librarians and their educator partners co-plan to support diverse learners. Working together professionally to decide what and how to teach empowers both the school librarian and educator because as collaborators they jointly create paths to academic success. The learners benefit from the instruction that results. Empowerment is a direct outcome of the transfer of individual control over learners' instruction to shared teaching. When the school librarian and educator revisit the lesson to evaluate its success, asking for input from learners exposes what went well and what should have been done differently. Asking for learner evaluation empowers learners to reflect on their own experience, enabling them to decide on strategies to use on their next assignment. Input from those most impacted by instructional decisions results in empowered learners.

## Information Specialists Empower

The school librarian serves as an information specialist by introducing educators and learners to technology tools that supplement school resources, assist in the creation of engaging learning tasks, connect the school with the global learning community, and provide access to library services (AASL 2018a, 14). By modeling instructional strategies, the school librarian empowers educators and learners to become effective users of the resources and research methods needed to accomplish their instructional goals. This approach emphasizes that "the school library supports individual responsibility for information use by providing an engaging learning environment that supports innovative and ethical use of information and information technologies" (AASL 2018a, School Library VI.D.2.). Key to learner and educator empowerment is that school librarians as information specialists provide for individual control over the learning process.

### Teachers Empower

One way for school librarians to empower learners is to give them opportunities to participate in library activities and initiatives. Creating learner-centered groups to elicit feedback about the school library encourages shared responsibility and buy-in. In addition, learners can assist in the implementation of library proposals. School librarians as teachers integrate the skills learners need to be ready for leadership roles within the school community. Empowering learners to be critical thinkers, enthusiastic readers, skillful researchers, and ethical users of information provides the foundation for responsible leadership and pursuit of personal and academic goals. School librarians foster active participation in learning situations by collaborating with other educators, encouraging open discussions with educators and learners, and allowing sharing of information created from analysis of their research. Learners and educators become invested in the school library learning experience as well as the school library through intentional conversations about library issues. Consciously teaching and then practicing principles of empowerment create opportunities for school librarians to embolden educators and learners while enabling these same skills in themselves.

### Program Administrators Empower

Some of the best opportunities for school librarians to practice empowerment come through the role of program administrator. Forming and updating strategic plans, library policies, and management procedures are examples of work for which the school librarian may seek stakeholder assistance. Organizing a committee that incorporates educators, learners, and community members permits diverse thinkers to share the work and responsibility. Stakeholders develop foundational understanding of updated documents when the school librarian incorporates their opinions, vision, and insight into plans, policies, and procedures. Program administration includes overseeing volunteers and managing clerical assistants. In doing so, the school librarian can empower others. When empowerment is carried out successfully, the outcome of shared responsibility is an efficient and well-managed school library that continually improves and achieves library goals.

## Connecting to the Shared Foundations

Google's second definition of *empower* is "make (someone) stronger and more confident, especially in controlling their life and claiming their rights."[1] School librarians foster the empowerment of stakeholders by the opportunities offered, skills taught, and resources utilized in the school library. The Competencies and Alignments in the Grow Domain of Include, Collaborate, and Engage in both the School Librarian and School Library Frameworks promote empowerment by emphasizing learner-initiated access to information, stimulating learners through discussion, and instilling responsibility for newly acquired knowledge. School librarians take a leadership role when they consciously facilitate empowerment to form relationships with stakeholders in the school library, resulting in longer lasting experiences and invigorating environments.

## INCLUDE

"School librarians explicitly lead learners to demonstrate empathy and equity in knowledge building within the global learning community by creating an atmosphere in which learners feel empowered and interactions are learner-initiated" (AASL 2018a, School Librarian II.D.1.). As instructional partners, school librarians need to advocate for learner choice when designing collaborative lessons with classroom educators because learners are more successful and invested in the school library when they can choose research topics or resources or both. Learner choice ranges from elementary learners being able to choose their own reading books rather than use a predetermined list to middle school learners choosing their own topic for a social studies project to high school students developing their own research question for an in-depth English research paper. Learners are also empowered when they are given a choice of products to display knowledge, ranging from elementary learners being encouraged to draw pictures instead of writing words to middle school learners using 3-D models to create symbols to represent new knowledge to high school learners creating skits or art projects to display research information. Empathy and equity are demonstrated because learners, being recognized as individuals, are choosing a topic and product based on their learning styles and interests rather than simply going through the motions of the assignment.

"The school library builds empathy and equity within the global learning community by ensuring that all learning needs are met through access to information and ideas located in a diverse collection of sufficient size for the learner population and supported by reliable hardware and software" (AASL 2018a, School Library II.D.1.). This School Library Alignment emphasizes the importance of the school library infrastructure and collection in extending empowerment. Choices made about collection development affect all stakeholders, from parents who want their learner to succeed with quality reading choices to classroom educators who use the resources to support curriculum. Learners, of course, are affected by collection development decisions by being able to locate resources that reflect themselves in the global learning community.

District- and building-level administrators make and monetarily support hardware and software decisions that affect the school library. Working with the administrator to evaluate hardware and software choices to make positive changes for the learners and school library is one of the school librarian's responsibilities as program administrator. For example, a secondary school utilized the library management system to create a report of "inactive" learners, those who had not checked out a book for two months. With this report, the school librarians were able to invite those learners for an exclusive "book tasting" event, during which the inactive learners were given first dibs on checking out new books. Because of this attention and the use of data to support learners, circulation rates increased, and everyone's needs were met. Sharing this event with the administration affirmed the decision to invest in that particular management software.

## COLLABORATE

"School librarians foster active participation in learning situations by stimulating learners to actively contribute to group discussions" (AASL 2018a, School Librarian III.D.1.). When learners are encouraged to share their voice, they are more invested and want to contribute to group discussions. To effectively meet this Competency, school librarians need to consciously ask themselves what is needed. What developmentally would stimulate my learners' needs to foster active participation? What does this active participation look like in order to achieve active and authentic contributions? Examples for younger learners could be formal and informal discussions about books, research topics, and new information found. Examples for educators as learners could be asking about and creating an online form for resource recommendations, resource utilization ideas, and instructional assessment ideas. When stakeholders realize that the school librarian is respectfully interested in their opinions, the level of participation in learning situations rises and becomes more beneficial to everyone involved.

"The school library supports active learner participation by creating and maintaining a learning environment that supports and stimulates discussion from all members of the school community" (AASL 2018a, School Library III.D.1.). The conscious decision of the school librarian to follow through with this ideal makes the school library a more welcoming and inclusive place. To take action on this ideal, school librarians need to form, organize, and lead an advisory board composed of different stakeholders—parents, administrators, classroom educators, learners, and community members. This advisory board is charged with holding quarterly face-to-face meetings to discuss collection development decisions, activities planned, and resources being used in the school library. With the school librarian as facilitator and program administrator, the advisory board becomes an active forum for stakeholders to share their perceptions, questions, and goals for the school library, all while listening to others' perceptions, questions, and goals. This advisory board, representing the different stakeholder voices, helps to expand the scope and value of the school library in the larger educational community.

## ENGAGE

Having learners become interested in and responsible for their interaction with information and its contribution to the school library is a consistent goal of school librarians. This goal is reinforced in the Competency, "School librarians support learners' engagement with information to extend personal learning by designing experiences that help learners communicate the value of the ethical creation of new knowledge and reflect on their process" (AASL 2018a, School Librarian VI.D.2.). The emphasis here is on giving the learner opportunities to show the value of the newly acquired knowledge and how it extends personal learning. For learners at all levels, being given the opportunity to create a book review (not a report) is a power-ful experience. A book review differs from a book report in that it contains authentic critiques of the book and its quality as a resource rather than a generic summary of the plot. Ranging from kindergarten students drawing pictures of their favorite part in a book to middle school students creating a video of their favorite scene in a book to high school students making a commercial for a book, the effect is the same. The learners are all communicating newly acquired knowledge and reflecting on how reading the book extended their personal learning. They all, whether consciously or unconsciously, want to share their ideas with the larger school community through the school library.

"The school library supports individual responsibility for information use by pro-viding an engaging learning environment that supports innovative and ethical use of information and information technologies" (AASL 2018a, School Library VI.D.2.). The key words in this Alignment are *innovative* and *ethical.* "The school library pro-vides a context in which the school librarian demonstrates and supports ethical behavior, and promotes the principles of intellectual freedom, information access, privacy, and proprietary rights" (AASL 2018a, 117). Fulfilling the roles of informa-tion specialist and program administrator, the school librarian searches for new, innovative resources for information and technologies to improve the stakehold-ers' learning. The results of the searching need to be shared with stakeholders in an appropriate manner. For example, administrators can make time during monthly faculty meetings for the school librarian to share new databases, websites, infor-mation technologies, and best practice instructional plans to incorporate into the classroom. The support of the administration and classroom educators for mod-eling and implementing the innovative and ethical use of information extends the role of the school library to the larger community.

# Taking Responsibility for Empowerment

Empowerment creates powerful results for the school library. School library outcomes are maximized when stakeholders share in library decisions and in the responsibility for achieving success. The opportunities to transform stakeholders into contributors are evident when school librarians serve as leaders, instructional partners, information specialists, teachers, and program administrators. These roles provide access points for school librarians to coach, mentor, and delegate tasks to learners, educators, and community members. When school librarians coach learners, they create "an atmosphere in which learners feel empowered and interactions are learner-initiated" (AASL 2018a, School Librarian II.D.1.). All learners and educators benefit from mentoring. Having a knowledgeable colleague to reach out to solves problems while developing relationships that foster self-confidence. Volunteers and clerical assistants are empowered through delegation of tasks. School librarians accomplish this goal by recognizing stakeholders' skills and then entrusting tasks to them in increasing levels of responsibility. Effective strategies such as coaching, mentoring, and delegating tasks develop stakeholders into confident, self-reliant individuals who are knowledgeable contributors to the achievement of school library goals.

The *Cambridge Dictionary*'s definition of *grow* is "to become more advanced or developed."[2] School librarians advance and develop learners', educators', and community members' commitment to the library through empowerment. Using the Competencies and Alignments from the Grow Domain of Include, Collaborate, and Engage in both the School Librarian and School Library Frameworks, school librarians have opportunities to sharpen their own empowerment skills as well as develop empowerment in library stakeholders. For example, in the Grow Domain, the School Library Alignment supports involving stakeholders by "clearly and frequently articulating the school library's impact when communicating with administration, faculty, staff, learners, parents, and the community" (AASL 2018a, School Library II.D.3.). Accomplishing this goal may result in empowering stakeholders through instructional planning, committee work, and volunteer opportunities. Collaborating and engaging with stakeholders requires effective and consistent communication of how, when, where, and why the school library positively impacts the school. By putting into practice each of the Competencies and Alignments in the Grow Domain, school librarians become more proficient leaders as they seek stakeholder engagement.

## NOTES

1. https://google.com
2. https://dictionary.cambridge.org/us/dictionary/english/grow

PART D: RELATIONSHIP BUILDING

## Reflection Questions

Provide thoughtful answers to the following reflection questions using the lines provided.

After meeting with educators and learners, how do the following questions provide analysis for guiding future interactions?
   a. What went well?
   b. What did not go well?
   c. What would I do different during the next interaction?

_____

_____

_____

How does self-awareness benefit relationship-building in the school community?

_____

_____

Why do I want to empower the school library stakeholders? How would this empowerment maximize the school library?

_____

_____

What other Shared Foundations, Domains, and Competencies or Alignments in the AASL Standards Frameworks for School Librarians and School Libraries can I apply to partnerships, self-awareness, and empowerment when building relationships? Explain how.

_____

_____

_____

## Self-Assessment

**Goal:** To self-assess and take action on my relationship-building objectives

Apply the following table to foster partnerships, self-awareness, and empowerment, using the professional learning goals as targets, the prompts to reflect on your practice, and the assessment criteria to structure improvement goals.

| Assessment of Relationship Building | Professional Learning Goals | Prompts | Assessment Criteria |
|---|---|---|---|
| **Partnerships** | • Foster stakeholder partnerships to build school library relationships. | • With which stakeholders am I choosing to make partnerships?<br><br>• Which school librarian role(s) best promote stakeholder partnerships? Why? | • I list specific stakeholders that I have reached out to for partnerships.<br><br>• I explain why and how different school librarian roles promote partnerships. |
| **Self-Awareness** | • Cultivate self-awareness to increase school library relationships. | • How does self-awareness foster building relationships?<br><br>• How does self-awareness influence my decisions about the school library? | • I list examples of times that self-awareness fostered building a relationship.<br><br>• I list specific examples of how my self-awareness influenced my decisions. |
| **Empowerment** | • Utilize empowerment to build stakeholder relationships. | • Why do I want to empower the school library stakeholders?<br><br>• Which strategy am I using to transform the school library into an empowering culture? | • I reflect on how I can empower the stakeholders.<br><br>• I list which strategy best worked to transform the school library into an empowering culture. |

## Breakthrough Skills

When building relationships, be proactive, ask clarifying questions, and choose a strategy to maximize partnerships, self-awareness, and empowerment. Incorporate these breakthrough skills into your practice to strengthen relationship building for the school library.

- **Be proactive** in building relationships, whether through partnerships or empowerment of stakeholders. When you are proactive, through different means of communication, in reaching stakeholders, the results are more effective. All types of stakeholders appreciate being sought out for opinions, questions, and ideas. Their investment in the school library strengthens and forms longer lasting relationships.

- **Ask clarifying questions** to build more self-awareness and authentic relationships. Clarifying questions help determine the why behind confidence building, decision making, and communication. With clarifying questions, the purpose of the partnerships becomes focused, the reflections from self-awareness assessments become clearer, and the result of empowerment widens to affect more people.

- **Choose a strategy** to develop empowerment. You need to realize which strategy—coaching, mentoring, delegating—best fits your management style in order to effectively empower stakeholders. Coaching and mentoring are done in both formal and informal situations, depending on the stakeholder. Delegating is done intentionally to build trust rather than micro-manage. Empowerment of stakeholders expands the role and instructional impact of the school library in the larger school community.

# CONCLUSION

Excellence is hard to achieve without a plan. A clear strategy guided by standards makes excellence easier to accomplish. The *National School Library Standards for Learners, School Librarians, and School Libraries* provides school librarians with an organized and comprehensive strategy to master professional excellence. The force behind school librarian excellence as leader, instructional partner, information specialist, teacher, and program administrator is experiencing these roles through the Domains of Think, Create, Share, and Grow. The roles and Domains dynamically combine to allow school librarians to personalize their growth by practicing, modeling, and communicating the Competencies and Alignments in these Domains. Incorporating the scope of the AASL Standards Integrated Frameworks into leadership development is a mandate for success for school librarians and school libraries. Through strategic thinking, decision making, communication, and relationship building, school librarians take responsibility for leadership growth that will positively impact future generations of learners.

# WORKS CITED

AASL American Association of School Librarians. 2017. "Best Apps for Teaching and Learning 2017." June 29. www.ala.org/aasl/standards/best/apps/2017.

————. 2017–2018. "Common Beliefs." *National School Library Standards.* https://standards.aasl.org/beliefs/.

————. 2018a. *National School Library Standards for Learners, School Librarians, and School Libraries.* Chicago: ALA Editions, an Imprint of the American Library Association.

————. 2018b. *National School Library Standards Implementation Plan.* https://standards.aasl.org/wp-content/uploads/2017/11/AASL_ImplementationPlan_2017.pdf.

"A Book Lover's Paradise." 2018. Library Hotel Collection. https://libraryhotelcollection.com/en/library-hotel.html.

ASQ American Society for Quality. 2018. "Fishbone (Ishikawa) Diagram." http://asq.org/learn-about-quality/cause-analysis-tools/overview/fishbone.html.

Bennett, Laura. 2013. "10 Conference Call Etiquette Tips You Should Strive to Follow." Eimagine. June 4. http://eimagine.com/conference-call-etiquette-tips-you-should-strive-to-follow/.

Bolman, Lee G., and Terrence E. Deal. n.d. "Reframing Organizations." www.tnellen.com/ted/tc/bolman.html.

Breedon, Thomas. 2018. "Lessons from a Year in Space." The Richmond Forum. November 17. https://richmondforum.org/scott-kelly/.

Brown, Tamiko. 2017. "5 Reasons School Librarians Should Use Social Media." EDU (blog). November 14. http://edublog.scholastic.com/post/5-reasons-school-librarians-should-use-social-media#.

Coach K. 2018. "Motivation." https://coachk.com/motivation/.

Conlon, Jerome. 2015. "The Brand Brief Behind Nike's Just Do It Campaign." *Branding Strategy Insider* (blog). August 6. https://www.brandingstrategyinsider.com/2015/08/behind-nikes-campaign.html#.W2NJD9JKhPY.

Cragg, Emma, and Katie Birkwood. 2011. "Beyond Books: What It Takes to Be a 21st Century Librarian." *The Guardian,* January 31. https://www.theguardian.com/careers/job-of-21st-century-librarian.

Cross, Robert. 2013. "Welness: PartnerMD—Resilience an Important Part of Physical Health." *Richmond Times-Dispatch,* December 2. https://www.richmond.com/life/health/welness-partnermd-resilience-an-important-part-of-physical-health/article_e3d2e059-05c7-53c0-bb7b-3644e5016a5d.html.

Davis, Vicki. 2018. "Amazon Alexa in the Classroom." *Cool Cat Teacher* (blog). April 13. www.coolcatteacher.com/amazon-alexa-classroom/.

DeMers, Jayson. 2017. "7 Steps to Compromising Effectively as a Business Leader." *Entrepreneur,* July 6. https://www.entrepreneur.com/article/296637.

*Deseret News.* 2015. "34 of the Best Lemony Snicket Quotes." *Deseret News,* February 27. https://www.deseretnews.com/top/3089/15/-34-of-the-best-Lemony-Snicket-quotes.html.

Dweck, Carol. 2015. "Carol Dweck Revisits the 'Growth Mindset.'" *Education Week,* September 22. https://www.edweek.org/ew/articles/2015/09/23/carol-dweck-revisits-the-growth-mindset.html?cmp=cpc-goog-ew-topics&ccid=topics&ccag=growth mindset&cckw=growth mindset&cccv=content ad&gclid=Cj0KCQjwv-DaBRCcARIsAI9sba8uGRpLLHI3RH_99FTlKG96vd7piiSZCThXJcf_eZOeKBM0bDn-hvoaAhT-EALw_wcB.

EBSCO. 2017. "Makerspaces: Hands-on Learning for Students of All Abilities." *EBSCOpost* (blog). August 30. https://www.ebsco.com/blog/article/makerspaces-hands-on-learning-for-students-of-all-abilities

Elmansy, Rafiq. 2018. "How to Apply Root Cause Analysis Using 5 Whys." Designorate. August 2. https://www.designorate.com/how-to-apply-root-cause-analysis-using-5-whys/.

Garson. 2017. "Tell 'Em What You're Going to Tell 'Em; Next, Tell 'Em; Next, Tell 'Em What You Told 'Em." Quote Investigator. August 15. https://quoteinvestigator.com/2017/08/15/tell-em/.

Harada, Violet H., and Joan M. Yoshina. 2010. *Assessing for Learning: Librarians and Teachers as Partners.* Santa Barbara, CA: Libraries Unlimited.

HCPS Henrico County Public Schools. 2012, June. "Policies and Regulations: Guidelines for Selection and Review of Instructional Materials." https://webapps.henrico.k12.va.us/policy/chapter.asp#R7-05-008.

———. 2018a. "Beyond the Shelf: HCPS Libraries: Growing Lifelong Readers, Transforming Learners; 2018 First Quarter Report." https://sites.google.com/henrico.k12.va.us/hcpslibraryhighlights/home.

———. 2018b. "Henrico Learner Profile." http://blogs.henrico.k12.va.us/hlp.

IRIS Center. 2018. "What Is Instructional Scaffolding?" The IRIS Center, Peabody College, Vanderbilt University. https://iris.peabody.vanderbilt.edu/module/sca/cresource/q1/p01/.

Khazan, Olga. 2016. "The Best Headspace for Making Decisions." *Atlantic,* September 19. https://www.theatlantic.com/science/archive/2016/09/the-best-headspace-for-making-decisions/500423/.

Lau, Joe, and Jonathan Chan. n.d. "What Is Critical Thinking?" Critical Thinking Web. https://philosophy.hku.hk/think/critical/ct.php.

Lloyd, Sam. n.d. "Managers Must Delegate Effectively to Develop Employees." Society for Human Resource Management (SHRM). https://www.shrm.org/resourcesandtools/hr-topics/organizational-and-employee-development/pages/delegateeffectively.aspx.

Mariama-Arthur, Karima. 2015. "Five Aspects of Body Language That Affect Business Communication." *Black Enterprise,* May 19. https://www.blackenterprise.com/body-language-tips-business-communication-office/.

Marr, Bernard. 2018. "How Much Data Do We Create Every Day? The Mind-Blowing Stats Everyone Should Read." *Forbes,* May 21. https://www.forbes.com/sites/bernardmarr/2018/05/21/how-much-data-do-we-create-every-day-the-mind-blowing-stats-everyone-should-read/#300276c460ba.

Martin, Ann M. 2013. *Empowering Leadership: Developing Behaviors for Success.* Chicago: American Library Association.

McCarthy, Niall. 2018. "America's Most and Least Trusted Professions" [Infographic]. *Forbes,* January 4. https://www.forbes.com/sites/niallmccarthy/2018/01/04/americas-most-and-least-trusted-professions-infographic/#421882a565b5.

Meyer, Robinson. 2018. "The Grim Conclusions of the Largest-Ever Study of Fake News." *Atlantic,* March. https://www.theatlantic.com/technology/archive/2018/03/largest-study-ever-fake-news-mit-twitter/555104/

Newberry, Christina. 2018. "23 Benefits of Social Media for Business." *Hootsuite Social Media Management* (blog). May 2. https://blog.hootsuite.com/social-media-for-business/.

Paul, Richard, and Linda Elder. 2008. "Defining Critical Thinking." Foundation for Critical Thinking. https://www.criticalthinking.org/pages/defining-critical-thinking/766.

Roberts, Kathleen R. 2018. "Perspective on Taking Initiative." Interview. July.

Salzberg, Sharon. 2015. *Real Happiness at Work: Meditations for Accomplishment, Achievement, and Peace.* New York: Workman.

Saylor Foundation. 2013. "The Benefits of Empowering Employees." https://resources.saylor.org/wwwresources/archived/site/wp-content/uploads/2013/02/BUS208-5.2-The-Benefits-of-Empowering-Employees-FINAL.pdf.

"Strengths: StrengthQuest Assessment." 2017. Virginia Tech. https://onecampus.vt.edu/task/all/strengths.

"The Importance of Face-to-Face Communication." 2013. *Ashton Insider* (blog). November 21. https://www.ashtoncollege.ca/the-importance-of-face-to-face-communication/.

Wachtel, Allison. 2012. "How Parcheesi Works." HowStuffWorks. February 15. https://entertainment.howstuffworks.com/leisure/brain-games/parcheesi2.htm.

Wellens, A. Rodney. 1993. "Group Situation Awareness and Distributed Decision Making: From Military to Civilian Applications." In *Individual and Group Decision Making: Current Issues,* edited by N. John Castellan Jr., chap. 14. Hillsdale, NJ: Erlbaum. https://books.google.com/books?hl=en&lr=&id=9mMOXnJTqowC&oi=fnd&pg=PA267&dq=concept of awareness in decision making&ots=RMKiCNS_Lf&sig=Y1Bm41MxX_tF19zUYMp115rE2wk#v=onepage&q=concept of awareness in decision making&f=false.

Wilhelm, Jeffrey. 2014. "Learning to Love the Questions: How Essential Questions Promote Creativity and Deep Learning." *Knowledge Quest, 42*(5), May/June.

"Written Communication." n.d. *Encyclopedia of Small Business.* https://www.referenceforbusiness.com/small/Sm-Z/Written-Communication.html.

# INDEX

*An italicized page number indicates an illustration.*